ENG & CHANG

FROM SIAM TO SURRY

"A JOURNEY"

BY

MELVIN M. MILES

Contact the Author at: melvin.miles1943@gmail.com

ISBN-10: 1490527508
ISBN-13: 978-1490527505

Revised

Dedicated To:

My Family
Sydney, Sage, Tamera, Derrick, and Grace

Also, to Betty Bunker Blackmon...
the great granddaughter of Eng Bunker, who has been a
great friend and an inspiration to restore the history of
Eng and Chang.

PROLOGUE

Hello. I am Melvin Miles. I have never written a book before, which will not be a surprise to you as you read this! Having grown up in rural Alleghany County, NC, I am the youngest child of four children. My family was as poor as "church mice," but we did not know that because everyone we knew was just as poor.

When I was in the eleventh grade at Sparta High School, I started a research project on "family history" for English. That was in the 1959-60 year. This is where I really discovered a "connection" on my dad's side of the family to the Siamese twins, Eng and Chang Bunker. Their manager and traveling companion was Charles Harris, who was from Ireland. He had traveled with them for many years, and was very instrumental in bringing them to Wilkes County, NC, via an invitation from Dr. James Calloway. This information was exciting for a while, then the project was laid aside while I was a student at Appalachian State Teacher's College, Boone, NC. During this time, my oldest sister, Vena, became interested in genealogy and did an extensive research of ancestors and descendants of my grandparents, John Thompson and Maryann Almeda McBride Miles. Vena continued this project for years and presented all of her information to each family attending a reunion that was held in 1989. Our family did not have another reunion until 2011 when my other sister, Betty, helped me collect numerous pictures and other pieces of history to complete a "power point" on our relatives. And again, "the Siamese twins" travel companion, Charles Harris, surfaced.

Our latest research also contained more information about Eng and Chang Bunker and their settling in Traphill,

4

NC. Once again, the project was laid aside until several years after my retirement from teaching, when I took on a fun filled job in Mount Airy NC, driving a Mayberry Squad Car and conducting tours of our area. Since the Siamese twins spent a greater part of their lives in Surry County, I became even more interested. This time I had a very real reason to research everything that I could find about the twins, in order to be able to answer questions that curious tourists might ask. The more I researched, the more I wanted to research. I did my first Eng and Chang Bunker presentation at the genealogical Society of Surry County in 2011. Much to my surprise, when I walked into the meeting, I was greeted by some guests who happened to be descendants of Eng Bunker. My first thought was, "What am I doing here? They will crucify me!" Well, from that presentation I have been very fortunate in developing a very close friendship with Betty Blackmon and her children—Tanya Jones, Deidre Rodgers, and Zack Blackburn, Jr. Betty is a great granddaughter of Eng Bunker. She now introduces me to her friends as her new cousin, Melvin Miles-Bunker. (I can only acknowledge that now I have earned the hyphen.)

Later in 2011, I was very "flattered" by being invited to speak at the 22nd Annual Reunion of the Descendants of Eng and Chang. This was also the 200th Anniversary of their birth. I will admit that I was a bit nervous. Very quickly I learned the meaning of feeling like "the preacher preaching to his choir." What could I possibly tell this group about their family that they did not know already? The family was very receptive with somewhere between 125-150 people present. I talked about Eng and Chang's travels from Siam (officially Thailand since 1949) to Boston, to New York, to world tours, to Wilkes County, NC, and to Surry County, NC. What I presented must have been of interest because I was invited back again as speaker in 2012. I made my presentation again with additional information and was "well received" again.

When I exited the stage, a descendant from Oklahoma came up to me and asked if I had all of this information written down anywhere. I told him, "No. It is just in my head." He told me that the information needed to be in a book. Well, I had never had such a thought. Then before leaving for the day, two additional descendants asked if I had ever considered writing a book. Well "CLICK, CLICK," the bells and whistles started going off in my head with the question, "Why not?"

So with the information that I have collected via computer, from my friend Betty Blackmon, a great granddaughter of Eng Bunker: from Tanya Jones, daughter of Betty Blackmon, who is the Director of The Surry Arts Council, which has a photo exhibit of Eng and Chang, and from Jessie Bunker Bryant who has compiled an excellent book entitled, The Connected Bunkers, Descendants of the Siamese Eng and Chang Bunker. Using the greatest factual book, The Two, written by Irving Wallace, and continuing with information from my old family records, I will attempt to recreate "my story" about Eng and Chang. Now as I am approaching my 70th birthday, I have decided that it is only fair to both me and the Bunker descendants that I leave a little bit of history as seen from an "outsider."

I give you this book for what it may be worth to you. I have enjoyed my research, and I can only hope that someone will continue with the history of this unique family consisting of two of the most widely known men ever to live.

Eng and Chang Bunker

From Siam To Surry

CONTENTS

The Beginning of Forever Together

There is no better place to start than at the very beginning.

The date was May 11, 1811...

The place was Siam, Province of Samutsongkram, in Southeast Asia, which would someday be known as Thailand. This was in one of the many river inlets near the village of Meklong, on a bamboo mat in a small houseboat. A birth was taking place, and the babies were going to become the world's most famous connected twins. Twin boys were born on Saturday, May 11, 1811. The father, named Ti-aye was Chinese and the mother, Nok was half-Chinese and half-Malayan. The mother was described as being 5'9," well formed, large hipped, and for her country, a strong woman. The births were number 5 and 6 of what would be 9 children born to this couple. The couple was hoping to have many more children because families with many sons and daughters enjoyed much respect in Siam.

This being the wet season, which came in May, the night temperature would average between sixty-five and seventy degrees, and the daytime temperature reached the nineties. The rains came and the humidity and the heat together made the entire countryside of rice lands and parched grass seemed more like that of an oven. The river waters would rise and carry with them the boats and "floating houses" made of bamboo covered with thatched leaves.

Since complications during delivery were very rare, there were no expected difficulties to occur for what Nok thought would be her fifth delivery. To everyone's surprise, she eventually delivered twins. This was a very unusual occurrence, and their arrival was a special occasion, calling for extra celebrations.

In the book, *Duet for a Life-time*, by Kay Hunter, the actual delivery of the twins was recorded as follows on pages 14-15.

The strange factor about these twins was that they arrived in the world simultaneously, and not one after the other as was the usual situation in a twin birth. They were small, even for twins, and when they were born the head of one of them was between the legs of the other one. The women who were assisting were taken by surprise at the unusual delivery, but after the first astonishment, they were lost in admiration for the two babies, who looked rather like a parcel that had been tied very neatly. For a second the infants lay very silent and still, and then they began to cry loudly. Relieved at the noisy signs of life, the women laughed and chattered together excitedly, and went to pick them up in order to wash them.

It was as they moved the babies that their chattering stumbled. The joy which had surrounded the birth suddenly died away and the silence fell as one after the other the women stared at the babies and realized that there was something unbelievably wrong. Both were boys, and each one was perfectly formed; two sets of tiny limbs waved helplessly above the two dark little heads. Everything was as it should be except for one defect. These two babies had not been entirely separated from each other. They were still joined at the chest by a large band of flesh, lying like a permanent bridge between them. Not having seen anything like this before, the peasant women were terrified, and they stared at the phenomenon with a mixture of fear and revulsion. They were afraid to touch the babies, and the whole situation was beyond their understanding. The whole deformity came as a spine-chilling shock to this region of superstition and fear of the unknown.

As the moments passed by, it became essential that something should be done for the two tiny crying boys who were still lying there awaiting attention. It was their mother who finally recovered herself sufficiently to take in the shattering event and reassure her friends. It was the natural reaction of a mother. These were still her babies, whatever they looked like, and there could be no possible harm in such small, dependent creatures, who she named Chang and Eng.

At birth the band which joined them was twisted, and they lay in opposite directions, but as the mother turned them carefully, so that they both lay the same way, with heads and feet together, the band straightened out and held them face to face. In the center of this pliable band was a single umbilicus, serving both babies. As they lay there, from the onlooker's point of view, on the left was Eng and Chang, who was slightly smaller, was on the right.

After this miraculous birth, the lives of the family would be changed forever. As infants, the Chinese Twins, as they were called, were very delicate, held face to face by their common ligament. They were extreme objects of curiosity. The local townsfolk who had heard of this strange birth came to see them. Visitors would travel great distances, crowding the riverbanks to see if they might get a glimpse of the two children who had been born joined together. As they grew, the villagers were gradually getting use to seeing them, and the curious travelers eventually stopped coming.

Eng and Chang being the first of what we now know as "Siamese" twins, only because they were born in Siam, were not the first recorded conjoined twins. But they were the first conjoined twins to be known over most of the world. In 1100 a double birth of this kind was recorded in Biddenden, Kent, where two sisters were born joined at the hips and shoulders. They became known as The Biddenden Maids and lived to be in their mid-thirties. Then there were The Scottish Brothers, who lived for twenty-eight years at the court of King James III of Scotland. And one would only suspect that there were other unrecorded cases.

With customs in Siam consisting of many sundry superstitions, anything out of the ordinary was guaranteed to bring panic, and the rumor was believed that the birth was an omen indicating the approach to the end of the world. An account of this unusual birth reached the King of Siam, Rama II, who was very disturbed, and he ordered that the two babies should be killed without delay. After the king learned that the two boys would probably grow up and be able to support themselves by working, and that they did not create any danger for him or to the world in general, he finally decided that they might grow into useful citizens and he permitted them to live. They were to remain with their parents on the houseboat.

Nok, their mother, was determined that they should grow up as normally as possible. She did not ignore the twins, nor did she pity and overprotect them. She was very "matter-of-fact" about them, and treated the two much as she treated her other children.

As to be expected, one of the very first difficulties they faced was in learning to walk. This was a major obstacle to Eng and Chang. Crawling was easy, but standing up was a challenge. At the time, walking forward seemed almost impossible. *American Pamphlet, October 1836,* described their initial efforts as: "Anyone who has ever seen two inebriated men, with locked arms, endeavoring to process in a fixed direction, may form some idea of their earliest efforts; but their mother has remarked that, after once becoming accustomed to the task of maintaining a proper center of gravity, their advance in the practice of pedestrianism was truly astonishing."

With massaging and exercise, the ligament stretched. From a face-to-face position as infants, Eng and Chang began to stand and move side by side. Usually one twin's arm was tossed over the other twin's shoulder. The flesh bond between them lengthened to 5 ½ inches. But still Ti-eye and Nok made no effort to have the ligament cut apart. The loving parents feared that such an operation might kill one or both of their children.

When the twins were growing up, they were each others best friend. It was noticed that they always seemed to prefer each others company to that of any other persons. Jokingly, their mother said, "they nearly always played together and so accustomed was I to this peculiarity, that whenever they became lost, I would only hunt for one of them, satisfied that when I found the one I would also find his brother somewhere in the immediate area.

Over the years, the twins learned to function as one and could coordinate with each others movements. They would often run to the top of a hill, wrap their arms around each other and roll down, laughing all the way. As they grew, the connecting band stretched to allow them to stand side by side. Eventually there was nothing these two young boys, in spite of being joined and short in stature, could not do, including swimming, running and playing. Also, they learned to paddle a boat at a very young age. When they were seven, Eng and Chang had received their first schooling. According to the *American Pamphlet, October, 1836:* "At an early age they received the usual amount of teaching that was given to the middling classes, and learned to read and write their native language with tolerable proficiency."

During the year, 1819, an absolute disaster devastated this family. A cholera epidemic swept through Southeast Asia. It hit the village of Mekong with all of its power. As Eng and Chang recalled the events to their American friend, Judge Graves. "The cholera came upon the inhabitants of Mekong in the most malignant form and no one knew of anything that would prevent it. There were no remedies, relief or no cure for it. The victims died suddenly. Those living were unable to bury the dead; the bodies were thrown into the river; the sluggish water did not remove the putrid mass stench that arose from the water."

When this horrible cholera first began, there were eleven members of this family, two parents and nine children. Immediately, three of the children died. In a few short weeks, two more children became ill with the plague and died. The father, Ti-eye, lay seriously ill. Finally, he died too. After these deaths, there were only five members left in this family, the mother Nok, the older brother Noy, an older sister whose name is not known along with Eng and Chang.

Even though the bodies of the siblings had been removed from the riverboat, what still remained was the father's funeral. This was an event that would never be erased from the minds of the twins who were only 8 years old.

(As recorded in the book, The Two, by Irving Wallace and Amy Wallace, page 25).

Although only eight, Chang and Eng trailed after their mother, brother, and sister into the courtyard of the Buddhist temple. The coffin that held the body of their father rested on a bier covered with cloth, six feet above the ground. The coffin itself was draped with a crimson cloth woven with gold. Above the bier was a canopy of white—the color of mourning—and the canopy was festooned with fragrant flowers.

When the prayer was done, the priest, accompanied by several other priests, moved slowly toward the coffin. Chang and Eng watched as the priests lifted a strip of cloth that was attached to the head of their father's coffin. The cloth was cut by the priests, and pieces of it were handed to Nok, to Noy, to the sister, and to Chang and Eng.

Now the priests lifted the coffin and moved it inside the temple. Chang and Eng were told that temple attendants were washing and purifying their father's corpse.

Meanwhile, combustibles were being thrown on the bier. At last the priests reappeared carrying the body, which they placed gently on the bier. A priest passed out lighted tapers to the mourners, then returned to the bier and set fire to it. He signaled for the mourners to put their burning tapers to the funeral pyre also. Soon flames surrounded it, licking upward toward the sky, engulfing the twins' father in a blaze of red. And then it was over, the cremation ended, their father gone forever.

The cost of the funeral of Ti-Eye left the family penniless, even though Nok felt it was all very necessary. There was no money, and no father in the family to earn money. Eng and Chang would never again get to be young boys. Immediately, they had to start work in order to help to support the family.

Their very first job was as peddlers in the floating market. This is where various goods were bought, sold, and exchanged entirely from small boats which crowded the river. Eng and Chang did rather well there because people were fascinated by them being joined together. Their customers were fascinated by these two small boys joined together and would stop to buy their wares. This job on the floating market lasted for some time, and then the boys became more ambitious.

Somebody taught the twins how to preserve duck eggs and this bit of knowledge prompted them to breed ducks for themselves for the purpose of obtaining eggs. Duck eggs were very much in demand in the area, so the twins were very successful in a new venture of selling duck eggs. They could sell over 10,000 duck eggs in a year. Of course, all of the money was handed to their mother in support of the family.

Eng and Chang had not been duck owners very long before they adopted one of the ducks as a pet. They trained this duck to come when called, and to obey certain commands. Many of the villagers use to gather to watch the performance.

Now the two boys had won their first phase of the battle with life. They came through their childhood to the age of twelve having mastered most basic accomplishments necessary for their day-to-day lives. As far as was humanly possible, Eng and Chang were just normal, two boys living as one and managing to have a very satisfactory life.

The Introduction of
Robert Hunter and Abel Coffin

The year was 1824...

This was the year that an adventurous Scot named Robert Hunter who had trade dealings with Siam, and for many years was the sole representative from Britain to trade in this county, caught sight of Eng and Chang. In those days the west bank of the river was mainly the residential area, owned by the wealthy citizenry who lived along the canals, or 'kalongs'. Bangkok was somewhat like Venice, and the principal mode of travel was by boat. One evening when Robert Hunter was returning home across the river, he thought he saw a strange animal swimming some distance away. He could make out what looked like four arms and four legs, surmounted by two heads, all moving through the water in perfect co-ordination. The twilight of the evening was beginning to blanket the river, and Hunter found it very difficult to see exactly what was going on. But without incident the small strange water creature climbed up on to a small boat, and Hunter realized that he was looking at two small boys, naked from the waist upward, and very thin. He also noticed that these two boys were joined together at the chest.

For quite some time he watched them from a distance, and then he drew nearer. Fascinated by their quick movements and their synchronization as they handled the boat and the oars, he decided to find out something about them, so he approached them in an effort to become friends.

A friendship evolved between the two small boys and the Scottish merchant, who also took an interest in the rest of the twins' family. Often, Hunter visited their floating home among the crowded waterways. In later years, when the twins were away from home Hunter used to report to their mother of the letters he received from them, and then write back to the twins with accounts of what was going on at home. Their mother was unable to read or write, so it was impossible for them to correspond with her directly, but letters indicate that Hunter acted as a link between the twins and their family for many years after they left Siam.

To use Eng and Chang as a commercial enterprise may have occurred to Hunter shortly after meeting them. Although his first move to make friends with them was no doubt prompted by sheer curiosity. It is virtually impossible to think at what stage the potential of becoming money makers entered his mind. It was very clear that he was thinking along those lines, of letting others view the twins as he had done. What is known for certain is that during the first year of their friendship he did seek permission from the government of Siam for them to be taken to England, but for what purpose there is no evidence. It may be presumed that the idea of putting them into 'show business' had already suggested itself to him.

The Thai Government refused its permission for the twins to travel to England, so Hunter had to bide his time. Since he was a very patient man, he believed that he would eventually get what he wanted. While waiting, he would talk with the twins about the wonderful life they could live in the Western world and they soon developed a desire to travel, and their mother, too, was almost convinced that it would be a great opportunity for her sons if they were allowed to leave home and go abroad.

During the next four years the twins got to visit with King Rama III at the Royal Palace of Bangkok. The king sent a special embassy to Indo-China and invited Eng and Chang to accompany it. They were thrilled with the experience of travel and the meeting with the outside world, and afterwards returning to earth with a 'jolt', going back to their business in the duck egg trade.

Now the earliest seeds of adventure had been sown, and the twins were developing great tastes for going places and doing exciting things. Their little trips out of their normal surroundings, combined with Mr. Hunter's persuasive accounts of life outside Siam were beginning to have an effect. They wanted to travel, and a restlessness and desire for change began to come over them.

The opportunity for fulfilling these desires did not present itself for some time, and the next event of great significance in the lives of Eng and Chang was that of a new acquaintance, Captain Abel Coffin, another Westerner who was an American. Mr. Coffin was a frequent visitor to Siam, and as Master of a trading vessel he spent a lot of time in India and the Far East. He home was in Boston and he happened to be a business associate and friend of Robert Hunter. At the age of thirty-seven, Mr. Coffin, was already successful. In 1829 he was in Bangkok for the purpose of selling firearms, which he had bought at an auction in Calcutta some months earlier.

Finally, after all of the patient waiting, Hunter could now see the means of getting Eng and Chang away from Siam. If the King would agree when approached again, and they could persuades the twins' mother to part with them for a time, he and his traveling America could take them to the West, personally, in Coffin's ship.

Hunter discussed the matter with Captain Coffin, who was quite agreeable to assist in taking charge of the twins, so with the plan of campaign carefully fixed in their minds the two men went to work on the financial details. They would pay for the boys on a fifty-fifty basis, and they would therefore share any profits made from them on the same arrangement, making sure that the twins had their share and that they received due care and attention during their journey.

Eventually, Hunter and Coffin convinced King Rama III that he could let the twins go to the Western world. The King liked Hunter and Coffin and appreciated the work that the businessmen had done in his country. He was also satisfied that Eng and Chang would be well treated.

After Captain Coffin had met the twins, he was in complete agreement with Mr. Hunter that this venture might well prove to be lucrative. Together, they approached the twins' mother with an offer to take the boys to America and England if she was willing to let them go. Mr. Hunter said that he would take complete responsibility for their personal safety and welfare, and Mr. Coffin was assured that the twins would be in good hands.

Now it was going to take more than just a few convincing words for their mother to agree for the twins to go. At first she refused to grant permission. She loved her children and had somewhat of a special responsibility toward Eng and Chang. Her first concern was that they were being asked to travel across the world, perhaps an unfriendly world that would not understand the difficulties and their physical handicap. They were now accepted in their own surroundings and had developed a great confidence in their dealings with other people. But there was no way of knowing how they would be accepted in a strange environment entirely different from the one that they had always known.

Also, there was another important factor to consider. The twins were now seventeen and they were also breadwinners. Immediately, Nok could not figure out how she could support the family without the help of the twins but she did not want to stand in their way if they were determined to travel with the sea merchants.

This matter was settled very quickly when Mrs. Hunter and Coffin made an offer to Nok of a lump sum of cash, and provisions for she and the family while the twins were away. Not only did she have to deal with the persuasions of the two gentlemen concerned, but also Eng and Chang themselves were very desperate that she should allow them to go. Finally, she agreed.

Departing Siam for a New World

The date was April 1, 1829...

Finally the day of departure from Siam had arrived. "Saying their good byes" to their family and friends was not easy for the 17-year-old twins. But they would return. Or would they?

Eng and Chang had boarded an American ship *Sachem*. They stood in the crow's nest on the main mast of the ship, scanning the sea around them and looking for any sight of land. With a voyage lasting for weeks ahead of them, the twins soon began to find life on board ship to be exciting and interesting. Very quickly they became favorites of the ship's crew. They listened to the orders being called out and often called orders out themselves. Each day they were learning new words, new phrases, and new sentences in English by listening and repeating. Soon they were already hoping that someday they could captain their own ship.

Weeks were very fast slipping into months as the *Sachem* sailed through the waters of the Indian Ocean and into the Atlantic Ocean. On August 16, 1829, the *Sachem* gracefully arrived into the Boston Harbor. The journey took 138 days. Eng and Chang left the ship with many memories of helping the ship's crew.

The Sachem, the ship that brought Eng and Chang to Boston in 1829

With Captain Coffin being both a worthy seaman and a skilled promoter, he planned to turn the Siamese twins into a special attraction for the city's 61,000 residents.

The first order of business was to show Eng and Chang the city of Boston. This was done, of course, by horse-drawn carriage. The twins rode through the streets gazing at the brick and stone buildings with glass windows, so different from the bamboo structures back in their home country.

Eng and Chang also provided doctors in Boston with a few surprises. Dr. John Collins Warren of the Harvard School of Medicine was the first to give the twins a thorough examination. He found the hard substance joining the boys to be about two inches long at its upper edge and bout five inches long at the lower edge.

It measured about four inches vertically and two inches horizontally, and could stretch to almost eight inches. The cord seemed to be made up of cartilage. The question at hand... could the boys be cut apart?

Dr. Warren did not entertain the idea for two reasons.

There could be continuous tissue in this attached ligament that would make surgery dangerous. And more importantly, he did not feel that Eng and Chang were psychologically ready for such an operation. Because of this, Dr. Warren would not consider separating the twins.

Very soon after arriving in Boston, Mr. Hunter and Mr. Coffin hired a Boston native, James Webster Hale, to help promote the twins in America. Mr. Hale was only ten years older than Eng and Chang. He became their friend for a lifetime.

Now in preparing for their premier exhibition in America, Hunter and Coffin rented a giant tent for this very special occasion. The tent was large enough to hold thousands of people. The price of admission was fifty cents, which was not a small price in 1829. But Robert Hunter and Abel Coffin knew they had a special show exhibit that was going to be very profitable for them.

Hunter and Coffin would not have anything to do with the first printing of the advertising signs made for the exhibition, as the twins were being advertised as THE MONSTERS. The wording was quickly changed to THE SIAMESE DOUBLE BOYS.

Finally, the opening of the first show was beginning. Men, women, and children came in large numbers to the tent eager to see Eng and Chang. Mr. James Hale was to open the session by giving background information about the twins. Someone was randomly selected from the audience to come to the stage to personally examine the ligament, and testify to the audience that the exhibition was indeed legitimate. Many people asked questions with an interpreter helping the twins. Some of the questions were more difficult, but the twins tried to answer.

Soon the twins were presenting their second exhibition in Providence, Rhode Island. They had decided that just answering questions was too dull. So they put together a new act. They were performing somersaults and back flips. They lifted volunteers from the audience into the air and carried them around. Then the twins would soon engage in a game of checkers with volunteers coming from the audience.

September 18, 1829, the people of New York were waiting to welcome Eng and Chang. James Hale had placed posters and signs everywhere. The newspapers had been alerted. Every day from nine in the morning until two in the afternoon, and again from six until nine in the evening, people poured into the Masonic Hall on Broadway to see the SIAMESE DOUBLE BOYS. The twins continued entertaining their audiences with light gymnastics.

During the next three weeks in New York City, several doctors examined them. Each reaching the same conclusion regarding separation, it was simply too dangerous.

After leaving New York City, the twins exhibited in Philadelphia for one week. A doctor there claimed that the separation was practicable, but that he was not willing to do the operation.

Eng was 5 feet 3 ½ inches tall, and Chang was an inch shorter, making up the discrepancy in height by having special shoes made for Chang. In the photographs taken of them in later life, it is more noticeable that despite this extra inch, Chang still did not manage to stand in such an erect position as Eng, his body having a tendency to tilt outwards.

With their trip to America already being considered a financial success, Mr. Coffin, Mr. Hunter, and Mr. Hale were now planning a trip to England. Eng and Chang enjoyed new sights and meeting new people, so there was no persuasion needed to convince the twins to travel again.

The trip to England was to be aboard the *Robert Edwards,* which proved very uncomfortable for the twins. While their business managers enjoyed first-class cabins and treatment, Eng and Chang were assigned much less than desirable accommodations. For 27 days the twins ate salt beef and potatoes and slept on a hard floor. Upstairs Mr. Coffin and Mr. Hale ate in the ship's dining hall and had private cabins with plush beds.

Mr. Coffin tried to cover this mistake by denying that the twins were also registered for first-class accommodations, yet he never could find them better quarters. This was the first time Eng and Chang had felt "used and abused," but it would not be their last.

After fourteen months of traveling in England, Scotland, and Ireland, the twins were back in the United States and being put right back to work by Mrs. Susan Coffin, wife of Captain Abel Coffin, who was now their new manager. Mr. Robert Hunter had decided to give up his partnership in the twins, so he sold his half-interest to Captain Coffin. In turn, Captain Coffin, who wanted to return to his commercial enterprises in the East Indies, had given control of Eng and Chang to his wife, Mrs. Susan Coffin, with Captain William Davis, Jr., as her assistant. Mr. James Hale was retained as the twins' business agent. Susan Coffin, being very busy with her social and family activities, ordered Mr. Hale to keep in touch with her through Captain Davis. Mr. Hale was very unhappy with this arrangement. He did not like the constant pressure he was under with such a full travel schedule. He had not spent time with his wife, Almira, and his children for a long time, and he desired some time with them. He did realize, however, that he could not spend time with his family until he could find a better working arrangement. They were to tour New York City, Philadelphia, Boston, and then set out to crisscross at least fourteen of the twenty states that made up this nation at that time. They would also be venturing into Canada and traveling to Cuba. All of this traveling proved to be a very lonely time for Mr. Hale and Eng and Chang. These years were very hectic and were not pleasant for either of the twins who had now become mature, sophisticated young men, and who no longer could be referred to as the "Siamese Boys."

With all of the traveling and new things that the twins were experiencing, the twins were beginning to become accustomed to the ways of the world, and were beginning to lose that first impressive faith they had once had in everything and everybody. They were beginning to no longer accept things at face value, but began to question situations concerning themselves that in their earlier days in the West they would never have dreamed of doing. They were beginning to develop a new self-confidence that they had never known before.

Problems for James Hale were now becoming very prevalent. Most of his difficulties were coming from undue pressure from his employer, Mrs. Susan Coffin. She even accompanied him on some of his travels to make his wife jealous. Very quickly, Mr. Hale was making preparations to leave his position as manager of Eng and Chang. He enjoyed the twins very much, but could no longer deal with Mrs. Coffin.

Very soon Mr. Hale wrote a letter to his friend, Charles Harris, who was living in a boarding house in Newburgh, New York. Mr. Hale had met Mr. Harris, an Irishman, while touring with the twins in England. When Mr. Harris came to the United States to seek his fortune, the friendship resumed. The two men corresponded regularly during the time Hale was on the road with the twins. It seemed that some recent correspondence from Mr. Harris to Mr. Hale stated that he was 'down on his luck,' and that he was planning to return to England. In an effort to persuade Mr. Harris from returning to England, and as he was worried about his shortage of funds, Mr. Hale had written to offer him a $100 loan. Mr. Hale had responded to Mr. Harris of his own plans for the future, which he had already confided to Mr. Harris.

First, Mr. Hale brought his friend up to date on his relationship with Mrs. Coffin. He said that he was going to quit working for Mrs. Coffin within seven months and take over as proprietor of an inn that he had purchased in Lynnfield, Massachusetts. In spite of his affection for Eng and Chang, Mr. Hale could not pursue the presence of Mrs. Coffin any longer.

Mr. James Hale in later years

With a successor to Mr. Hale being needed immediately to manage the twins, he knew someone who was not only very competent to do the job, but also one who was in need of work. So Mr. Hale recommended his friend, Charles Harris, to become the new manager of Eng and Chang.

Very shortly Mr. Harris met with Susan Coffin for an interview, which went very well and a contract was signed between the parties. The contract stated that Mr. Harris would be paid . . . the sum of Fifty Dollars per month, for the time he is employed in the services of attending the youths. . ."

There is no evidence that the change of management troubled the twins in any way. They had become used to James Hale, very dependent on him, and they cared about him. Also, they had known Charles Harris socially and liked and respected him. Mr. Harris, born in Ireland, was thirty years old when he took over the twins. Although trained as an accountant, he listed himself as a doctor in a passport in 1835. In fact, the twins always addressed him and referred to him as "Doctor."

Finally with a fond farewell, Mr. Hale left to rejoin his wife and their two children, and the twins set off with Charles Harris to resume their tour.

Mr. Harris, being a prolific letter writer, bombarded Captain Davis with communications for Mrs. Coffin. In each letter he was very detailed in giving the summaries of their travels, their business, and the needs and activities of Eng and Chang. His letters were almost like diaries. He would start a letter in one town, giving all of the 'happenings' there and complete the letter in the next exhibit. Often, Mr. Harris passed on the good wishes of

Eng and Chang to the many friends they had made in Newburyport. And, he would also remind Mrs. Coffin to send them specific items of clothing.

Mr. Harris was continuing very explicit details in his letters concerning the twins and their 'needs' in his correspondence which took place during the next several months. Eventually, both bitter and angry letters were being exchanged as the twins were traveling from place to place. The twins asked for a raise to three dollars a week in their travel allowance. Their carriage needed maintenance. It seemed that Mrs. Coffin wanted all of the money that she could get and keep Eng and Chang on a 'barely survival' budget. The twins endured this knowing that it would not be long until May 11, 1832. This would be a big day in their lives. They would be twenty-one years old. They would legally be of age, and for the very first time have the legal right to determine their own future. Secretly, they had been plotting their future plans with both Mr. Harris and Mr. Hale.

They waited until June 1, 1832, when Eng and Chang declared themselves free of any management with Captain Abel Coffin, which included his wife, Susan Coffin. They felt that they had fulfilled the agreement made in Siam over the three years before, and now they were free to pursue their own futures. If they could not cut the band of flesh that conjoined their bodies, they certainly hoped to totally cut their ties with the Coffins. To celebrate their new freedom, they purchased and gave away 500 cigars.

A complete separation from their partners came with a great deal of difficulty. The partners reflected much anger and bitterness through correspondence. Captain Coffin claimed that he had handled the twins fairly. Eng and Chang disagreed. Both the Captain and Mrs. Coffin had brought much unhappiness into the lives of the twins. The twins always suspected the captain of swindling them out of a large amount of money.

Dr. Harris kept Eng and Chang busy. They traveled throughout the eastern United States. Sometimes they were playing to an extremely large crowd and sometimes to a lesser sized crowd. The size of the crowd often depended on the local economy. They toured almost every village and city in New York State. They covered New Jersey, Pennsylvania, Virginia, and Ohio.

When Eng and Chang traveled into the South, the size of the audience became much larger. In Tennessee and Alabama, the twins pulled in $1,105 in one month. When they continued on into Mississippi in the same year, they reached a total of almost $2,500.

The twins seldom heard from their mother back in Siam, but they always welcomed any news that they did receive. Late in 1833, Mr. Hunter visited Nok. Eng and Chang learned that their mother had remarried to a fisherman named Sen, and that all were in good health, including the brother and sister. The twins wrote to their friend, Mr. Hunter, in the spring of 1834 saying, "We are fully determined to go back to Siam but cannot at present fix anytime."

The longer Eng and Chang stayed in the United States, the more they liked the country. Since their 21st birthday in 1832 and employing their own manager, the twins had been very busy touring the eastern United States and continued bitter correspondence with the Coffins. James Hale, their former manager, had kept in contact with the twins and in December, 1834, he came from Boston to

Charleston, West Virginia to meet with them and visited for nine days. He then left for Cuba to make arrangements for Dr. Harris and Eng and Chang to join him later. The twins then left to exhibit in Savannah, Georgia.

On January 14, 1835, the twins accompanied by Dr. Harris, sailed for Cuba. They were on the ship for ten days before arriving in Havana where Hale was waiting to accompany them to their hostelry.

Mr. Hale had mounted an extensive advertising campaign for Eng and Chang while in Havana. He, of course, had to have handbills printed in Spanish. The trip proved to be very successful financially. One thing that Dr. Harris had not anticipated and was the language in Cuba being Spanish. The twins could only speak English and Siamese, so Dr. Harris had to employ an interpreter for the duration of their exhibit to answer spectator questions, etc. They even added a special feature to their act and that was puffing Cuban cigars that they both had learned to love. The people always applauded wildly causing Eng and Chang to ask for some Cuban rum as well. They enjoyed their time in the city like any other tourist.

In October, 1835, after much planning, Eng and Chang, accompanied by Charles Harris, left the United States with an itinerary of bookings that would include touching on England and six months in France, Belgium, and Holland. They arrived at Dover, on the English Channel, on November 22, 1835. They had a very busy and yet successful extended tour and left Holland, along with Harris, for their return trip to the United States on June 15, 1836. They arrived in New York City on August, almost eight weeks later.

For the next three years, Eng and Chang and Dr. Harris continued to tour through the eastern and southern portions of the United States. They toured day after day and town after town, taking in money and saving as much as they could, while at the same time they were facing smaller audiences. They were beginning to think in terms of working for the day when they could finally be free of the routine of one-night stands and public display. They shared a mutual secret desire to change the means of their livelihood. They were definitely entering a crossroad in their lives.

The big decision would soon come concerning their future and that would be to decide whether or not to return to Siam or to remain in the United States. This would occur in the place where they opened this last phase of their most continuous eight-year tour. The place was Peale's New York Museum, under the ownership of Rubens Peal, son of the founder of America's foremost theatrical showcase before the beginning of P. T. Barnum. Here, they would soon meet the individual who would be responsible for changing the entire direction of their lives in the years to come.

Not a Man but Men - 21st Birthday

The date was June 1, 1832...

In a letter to Robert Hunter who was in London, saying "Now that we have reached the age of 21, we are no longer under any arrangement with Captain Coffin. We have fulfilled all the engagements entered into between the Captain and ourselves back in Siam." Eng and Chang felt that they had fulfilled the agreement made in Siam over three years before, and were ready to pursue their own futures.

It is very clear that Eng and Chang had no second thoughts about terminating their employment with Captain Coffin. They were happy to be 21 years old and finally able to become "their own men".

In the years that followed, many biographers of Eng and Chang stated in various articles, pamphlets, and books, that the twins broke with the Coffin's because they had defrauded them, robbing them of portions of their box-office receipts. It was also known that Captain Coffin owed the twins' mother a second payment of $500 for their services, which he never paid to her, and Mrs. Coffin kept many of their personal things after they left; so, there is really no question except that the Coffin's did swindle Eng and Chang. Even though James Hale and then Charles Harris handled all of the monies collected and paid out to the twins, they only sent the profits on to Mrs. Coffin. The problem was in the fact that when the twins asked for extra allowances or expense funds, they were never granted. They believed that their employers were profiting out of proportion to their earnings. The twins felt as though they were being 'ruled and controlled' by other humans. Also, they felt like second-class citizens. So the twins ended the contract, mainly because they believed that it would be within their legal rights to do so. For this reason alone, on June 1, 1832, in Buffalo, New York, all ties had been cut from their past and they were now self-employed beings who would reap their own profits.

Their first act of business in their new life was to retain the services of their manager, Charles Harris. He knew his job well and the twins wanted to maintain him as their manager. Likewise Harris liked the twins a lot. He stayed with them as their manager throughout the next eight years of their tours, both American and foreign.

The next act of business was to make arrangements to purchase the horse, carriage and baggage wagon from Mrs. Coffin. An agreement was finally reached to close the purchase for $103. The twins had the money, so Charles Harris sent her a check and the twins had regained their possessions.

At last, the twins were ready to begin work. Their earnings would now belong to them. They were prepared to work harder because they felt that they would be paid "what they were worth." After covering almost every village and town in New York State, they spent the remainder of the year traveling in New Jersey, Pennsylvania, Virginia, and Ohio.

An interesting notation in Charles Harris' record books for the last day of June was Mr. Doty's bill, Seneca Falls for $12.75. Eng and Chang later knew a Dr. Edmund

H. Doty as the result of their close friendship with three brothers, William, Bethuel, and Frederick Bunker, all tea and wine merchants whose firm was Bunker & Company at 13 Maiden Lane in New York City. Because of the friendship, Eng and Chang allowed Bunker and Company to do much of their business and banking for them. One of the Bunkers had a daughter named Catherine, with whom Chang had fallen in love with on the twins' first visit to New York City. When Chang drew up his earliest will, he named Catherine Bunker as his major heir. Catherine Bunker eventually, married Dr. Edmund H. Doty. This did not end Chang's affection for Catherine which now included friendship with her husband. In 1849 Doty signed the twins for a tour. It is now very possible that "Mr. Doty" in Seneca Falls and Dr. Edmund H. Doty was the same individual.

During the remainder of 1932, the twins, along with Harris, were keeping themselves very busy with their travels and their exhibiting. However, Captain Abel Coffin and Susan Coffin and her assistant Captain Davis were still upset over the separation of Eng and Chang and much correspondence was continuing to be exchanged. Eng, Chang and Harris were looking forward to meeting with Captain Coffin in person, as soon as possible when Coffin returned to Boston. Eng and Chang wanted to vent all their grievances off their chests, while Harris only wanted to have Coffin audit his bookkeeping. Then they could all be finished with the Coffins. This feud continued between the twins and the Coffin's until August 28, 1837, when Captain Abel Coffin of Boston died of a fever at the Island of St. Helena.

Their lives continued by traveling, performing, moving from one place to another, and continuing to astonish their audiences with their now perfected act, which was witty, agile, and totally entertaining. The first shock of their appearance was beginning to wear off and audiences were now accepting them as entertainers rather than as oddities. People were beginning to forget that they were joined together, and were enjoying their shows because they were lively and amusing. This is what Eng and Chang had long wanted from an audience.

Even though they were making money rapidly, they were becoming very comfortable with their tours as strenuous as they may be. They had achieved the "performance" they wanted and they lived very well. They enjoyed both the fame and well-being which went along with being top artists. In spite of all of the fame which they had earned for themselves, they had remained both good natured and maintained a great sense of humor.

They could *ad lib* with the best comedians and their audiences loved it when they would stop from the stage to include the audience in their act. At one of their shows they asked that an audience member be refunded half his admission money. The theater manager was called into the act and when the manager demanded to know why he had been summoned the twins told him that this man only had one eye, so therefore they maintained he could only see half as much as the other guest in the theater. The manager complied with the request and there were bows and handshakes all around. The audience even stood and acknowledged their approval with an arousing applause.

Even though so much of this new idea of including the audience in their act was happening, it was nothing more than mere showmanship.   And it continued to happen for a very long time when the twins felt the necessity to arouse the audience. Eng and Chang were very often generous in their actions even when there was no audience present. They were very sensitive to reactions on visitors' faces and yet they were very quick to express opposition against disgust or patronizing looks. Also, they did not tolerate members of the audience who wanted to poke or probe them to make sure they were genuinely two individuals who were conjoined.

Once in Philadelphia a man squeezed Chang's hand a little too hard. Chang who was always the more quick tempered of the two, struck the man. The gentleman was furious, and applied for an Assault and Battery Warrant. Unfortunately for the man involved, he did not meet with the success of the doctor who had been attacked. The magistrate told the man that he could have a warrant for Chang, but this would also mean arresting Eng. This in turn put the magistrate in the awkward position of having to make a false arrest because Eng was innocent! The offended gentleman then decided that it may be better to just drop the matter. This was the end of this incident.

In the meantime, Eng and Chang were traveling through the South; Tennessee, Alabama, and Mississippi, where their profits soared. Later they were traveling to Louisiana, up and down the East Coast, Cuba, back to New York, Maryland, Virginia, England, France and the list continues.

During the next three years from 1835-1839, they continued touring throughout the eastern and southern parts of the United States. They were going into town after town, city after city, working very hard trying to earn all of the money they could but their audiences were starting to decrease in size. So many of the people had already seen them and did not care to return to a second appearance.

As a result of the twins beginning to make less money on their road tours they were now spending more time exhibiting at the Peale's Museum in New York. In fact now that they were not touring on the road as much, they had made over a dozen appearances at various Peale's Museums in New York City, Philadelphia, Albany, and Baltimore. Sometimes they may exhibit for as long as one month in one location, and sometimes they may exhibit as long as three months.

While Eng and Chang were on exhibition in the New York City Museum, there was a visit from a Southern physician from North Carolina who was in New York on business, had some free time in his schedule, visited the museum, saw the twins exhibit and became very fascinated with their being conjoined. He managed to visit with the twins in their dressing room. The twins did not realize that visiting with this gentleman would change their future forever. The exhibitions which had become their way of earning their living were going to stop. A completely new life with many unexpected ventures was lying ahead for Eng and Chang. Could they accept the challenge?

The Life Changing Influences from a Southern Gentleman

The year was 1839...

At one of the showings in Peale's, New York Museum, where the Siamese twins were exhibiting, there was a very nice Southern physician visiting New York from his home state of North Carolina. The physician was so impressed by the twins, not only by mere oddity, but also by their personalities and intelligence that he was determined to meet them on a personal basis. After viewing their exhibition, the physician asked an attendant if he might have the honor of meeting Eng and Chang. Very surprisingly to the physician, permission was granted.

Eng and Chang had already gone to their private dressing room when the physician introduced himself as Dr. James Calloway, of Wilkesboro, North Carolina. He was a grandnephew of the great frontiersman Daniel Boone. Dr. Calloway had served in the North Carolina legislature at the age of twenty-three, had studied medicine at the University of Pennsylvania, and had set up his medical practice in Wilkesboro. This medical practice ranged over seven counties in North Carolina. Later he became an officer in the Confederate Army and a stalwart of the Episcopal Church in Wilkesboro, North Carolina.

Dr. Calloway sat in the dressing room in Peale's Museum and became very deeply involved in a friendly conversation with Eng and Chang—not as abnormalities of nature but as human beings. Soon, the twins made it known that they went on a hunting or fishing vacation twice a year. This presented a great opportunity for the Doctor to express to the twins the many hunting and fishing opportunities that were available in Wilkes County located at the base of the Blue Ridge Mountains in Northwest North Carolina. He told the twins of all the many clear water streams with their 'fine' fishes; that the hills and mountains were plentiful with its larger game of deer and turkey galore as well as smaller game of squirrels and quail. Finally, Dr. Calloway invited the twins to come to Wilkesboro on their very next vacation. This was the beginning of a friendship that would last . . . ." The twins consulted with Dr. Harris and agreed to accept the physician's invitation. And, together the three arranged to spend their free time in Wilkesboro.

After exhibiting in North Carolina earlier in 1839, Eng and Chang were ready for a long vacation. They dimly remembered having exhibiting there at the place Dr. Calloway so vividly described as his corner of this great state. The twins had appeared in Wilkesboro, located in Wilkes County, where "For One Day only The UNITED BROTHERS, CHANG-ENG" received "Visitors at the tent - Admittance 50 Cents." But at that time Wilkesboro had been just another 'hamlet' where wide-eyed faces came to gather around them, to gawk and stare.

Soon and very soon the twins were on their way to Wilkesboro, not having any idea of the effect this visit would have on the remainder of their lives, all three of them.

With Eng and Chang arriving in this isolated and untamed northwestern corner of the state, without pressure of being exhibited, just being onlookers, Eng and Chang saw the area through a very different set of eyes. Yes, they were curiosities. They were even considered freaks by some. They were Orientals and probably the first to ever come into Wilkes County. But, to the majority they were just welcomed guests and human beings.

In turn, the twins found the people of Wilkesboro to be very friendly and generous. They felt that the people were very appreciative of the same values that they themselves held in high regard. And as for the landscape, with the beautiful Blue Ridge Mountains in the background, valleys, forests and rivers, all of this offered them their first opportunity to enjoy a peace and tranquility along with the promise of such sports as fishing and hunting.

In an unpublished manuscript, the twins' friend Judge Jesse Graves recounted their coming to Wilkesboro and the early days of their vacations:

> Mr. Chang and Mr. Eng . . . having traveled over most of the United States and much of Europe and having been for eleven years constantly before the public began to grow weary of that way of life and to wish for some rest and retirement. In this frame of mind they arrived at the quaint village of Wilkesboro (North Carolina) nestled down on the banks of the Yadkin River away up among the mountains traversing the western part of North Carolina. Captain Carmichael, a most agreeable, entertaining and accommodating host dispensed the comforts of his well supplied table most elegantly' and his excellent brandy purely distilled from the best applies in the world, was not without its charms of Dr. C. Harris who knew how to appreciate the luxury of the bowl. So, partly from their own inclination and partly at the instance of their old and long tried friend, the Doctor, it was determined they would spend an indefinite time in that retreat. Deer abounded in the

neighboring mountains, foxes in the fields around the village, and perch in the clear streams of the valleys, and in the brooks on the mountains the beautiful speckled trout were found in great abundance.

Fishing had been a sport and a business in which Chang and Eng had delighted in early life they had now become very expert in the use of fire arms, and had acquired a great fondness for hunting. Being now in a situation to engage in chasing stag and catching trout, they determined to remain at least until winter to enjoy the recreation which they had desired to find far away from the hurrying crowds.

Dr. Harris and the twins rented rooms from a Captain Carmichael who owned a hostelry in Wilkesboro. Soon they extended their stay. It was beginning to dawn on them that they did not want to leave Wilkes County. They did not want to return to Siam. They did not want to go back to touring the United States. Wilkes County had become the closest thing they had found to a haven, and all three of them wanted to make it their home. They had accumulated savings of over $10,000 which was a large sum at that time, but it was not enough for them to retire on. After all they were only 28 years old, healthy, energetic, had a very strong work ethic, and they desired absolute financial security.

Once the twins and Harris decided to stay in Wilkes County, it was time for them to find a more permanent place to live. While visiting in the Traphill community of Wilkes County, Dr. Harris and the twins were able to meet a friendly local merchant and farmer whose name was Robert Bauguess. When inquiring about the possibility of finding rooms, Bauguess just happen to have two available. Dr. Harris rented one of the rooms and Eng and

Chang rented the other. This would especially change the life of Dr. Harris forever.

Harris, age 38, soon found that his landlord had a daughter named Fannie. She happened to be single and the doctor found her to be more captivating than the good cheer of the host at the village hotel. Immediately, Harris' heart went out to Fannie Bauguess. A romance developed very quickly and ten months later Charles Harris married Fannie Bauguess. According to the custom of the people of that community, a great feast, or real marriage supper, was made and all the friends for several miles around were invited to come and witness the ceremony and partake of the good things provided for this great occasion.

Of course, among those present to see their friend and manager entering matrimony were Eng and Chang. Also attending as guest were two of the most sought after and popular young women in the community. These young women just happened to be sisters. Sarah Yates, usually called Sally Ann or Sallie, who was eighteen years old, and Adelaide Yates, known as Addie, who was seventeen, both daughters of David Yates and Nancy Hayes Yates, a very prosperous farmer who had a handsome white house and cabins for his fifteen slaves on a hill overlooking the Valley of Mulberry Creek.

Eng and Chang had met David Yates a few months earlier, but they had neither seen nor met his daughters. Toward the end of the wedding feast for the Harris' the twins introduced themselves to Sallie and Adelaide Yates, to whom they had been attracted. From the book, The Two, by Irving and Amy Wallace, pages 167-168, there is an account of the actual conversation from their introduction.

An account of their initial conversation has survived in a book privately published in 1936 in Burnsville, North Carolina, written by Shepherd Monroe Dugger, who as a young man had met the twins. Dugger's account reflects the tone of the twins' conversation, which was frequently impudent and humorous. According to Dugger, once the introduction had been effected, "a lively conversation" ensued.

Eng addressed Sallie and Adelaide Yates. "My brother wants to marry," he said cheerfully, "and if any young lady here will have him, we will have a wedding today." "It is he who wants to marry," said Chang quickly, pointing to his attached brother, "and he is putting it off on me just to raise a conversation with you about love. He'd marry at the drop of a hat, and drop it himself, if he could get the ugliest girl in town to say 'yes.'"

"The reason I don't marry," added Chang, "is because I'm fast to him. Isn't it a pity that neither of two brothers can marry, because he is fast to the other?"

"Indeed it is," answered Sallie Yates solemnly. "Is there no chance for you to be separated?"

"The doctors say not," said Eng, "and each of us decided that we would rather look on pretty girls, with a lean and hungry love-look, and continue to want a wife than to be in our graves."

Now Adelaide Yates spoke up. "What a pity that you who love ladies so dearly can't marry and those two young ladies can't have such lovely husbands as you would have been."

There was lulling in the conversation. There seemed little more to be said.

"Good-by," said the Yates sisters.

"Good-bye" said Chang.

Eng offered a promise. "Good-bye, my brother will be back to see you some day.

"If I come back," said Chang quickly, "I will leave him behind, because he always monopolizes the conversation of the girl I love best.

Eng was not through. "To show that I want to be fair," he said lightly, "I will let him take the choice of young girls now, and if we get back, the other shall be no less a choice to me."

Chang made his choice. He pointed to Adelaide Yates. On this, "they parted joking." Chang and Eng watched the Yates sisters make their farewells to Harris and his guests. Years later, Chang and Eng recollected the leave taking for Judge Jesse Graves, who wrote it down:

"In the morning the guests all departed, each taking his way home, Chang observed that a rather handsome young fellow dashed up beside of Miss Adelaide as she cantered off on the prancing bay; and Eng saw that a rather good looking young Methodist preacher, named Colson, rode more soberly along by the side of Miss Sally. If any emotion of interest stirred the breast of any of the parties at that time it is one of the unrevealed secrets."

But according to the story as told by the twins' 1936 historian, an "emotion of interest" did stir both Chan and Eng. Once alone in their bedroom, Chang brought up the Yates sisters.

"We will keep in touch with those girls," he said, "for they think more of us than we are thought of by all else in America."

Eng was less certain. "Maybe you are mistaken. It was only an acquaintance, and they did not want to render things unpleasant by bluffing our familiarity."

"It was more than that," said Chang earnestly. "I felt the thrill of their sympathy deep down in my soul. Maybe they will marry us."

Eng, ever aware of their condition, refused even to entertain the thought. "Marrying with us is a forlorn hope," he said. "No modest girl is apt to marry, where the pleasures of her bridal bed would be exposed, as ours would have to be."

"Brother, you see it wrong," Chang persisted. "It is the refined—and those only--who can excuse whatever is necessary to become a mother. We are not responsible for our physical condition, and we should not have to die childless on that account. We will see again, the dear girls who talked so good to us today and, through their love we may have children to carry our blood and image in the world, when we and their mothers have gone to the Glory Land."

But Eng remained cynical. "Brother, he said, "I never saw you so great a philosopher as you are now. Those girls inspired you and when you go back to see them, don't fail to take me, and I will do my best in helping you win Adelaide, who sent that thrill to the bottom of your craw. I know you have sand enough in your gizzard to digest it."

Before the end of 1839, the twins had bought about 110 acres of land in the Traphill community of Wilkes County. This was the first deed ever signed there, and they paid for their land with a bag of silver. They built a two-story house there which is still being lived in today.

First home of Eng and Chang in Traphill, NC, 1839

The twins' house contained only four rooms, two downstairs and two upstairs. A giant five-foot-wide chimney serviced all four rooms. Windows in each room stretched almost from floor to ceiling. Eng and Chang loved sunlight. The staircase leading from the ground floor to the second story was made extra wide, so that the twins could go up and down without difficulty. The kitchen, containing another huge fireplace, was built next to the house. Also, a horse stable, as well as a house for some slaves was erected.

By June 1840, the house was ready for occupancy. This house came to be called the Traphill house. While their house was built with local materials, the brothers delighted in ordering furnishing from New York City. They had seen many fine items on their touring ventures. They even hired Dr. Harris to bring rugs, candlesticks, framed pictures, silverware, and everything else needed to complete a home. Harris spent a total of $467 for these items. The beds, tables, and double-sized chairs were either custom-made or bought in Traphill or Wilkesboro.

It was very difficult for Eng and Chang to think of anything except their love for Sallie and Adelaide Yates. They busied themselves by clearing their land of stone, brush, etc. then plowed and planted their crops. They had also purchased horses, cows and pigs.

On November 15, 1842, Kay Hunter wrote in her book *Duet for a Lifetime*, that Eng and Chang wrote of their situation to Robert Hunter who was once again back in London: "We have bought some land in this country, and raise our own corn and hogs—we enjoy ourselves pretty well, but have not as yet got married. But we are making love pretty fast, and if we get a couple of nice wives we will be sure to let you know about it."

In the same letter, Eng and Chang went on to say that they lived near the Blue Ridge Mountains, twenty-five miles from the Virginia border and 180 miles from the nearest railroad. "So we are quite removed from the march of intellect," they wrote.

In order to keep up with the intellect, Eng and Chang continued to see their former manager and close friend, Charles Harris, and his young wife Fannie, who had recently given birth to their first child, a boy named Joseph. The Harris' had a house not far from the twins, located in a valley between the Blue Ridge Mountains and a large granite mountain known as Rock Mountain. Harris had resumed his original profession as an accountant.

Harris, being such a close friend of the twins, was someone with whom they were able to pour out their hearts. They told him of their love for the Yates sister and their secret desire to get married. To Harris, the idea of the twins, bound together by a five-inch ligament, actually marrying two normal young women seemed too bizarre—an invitation to disaster—always sharing meals, chores, even a bed with two men . . .

So far, Eng and Chang had not let the Yates sisters know their true feelings. But, at last they decided to do so. Just how far they could press their good fortune remained to be seen. It was obvious to both Eng and Chang, and to the Yates sisters, that any serious friendship between them was not going to meet with the approval of the local people in the area. Because they were afraid of what people would say, they kept their meetings secret. For a long time nobody knew that the twins were courting Sarah and Adelaide Yates. Having succeeded in keeping their affairs secret for what seemed to be a very long time, the twins became bolder and decided that the time had come to put matters on a more open basis. For the past four years, Eng and Chang had simple called on the Yates sisters at their parents' home. They had never been seen in public. The serious pursuit of the Yates sisters by Eng and Chang had been a secret known only to the four of them.

That changed one Saturday afternoon when the foursome climbed into a buggy and rode the six miles from the Yates' farm into Wilkesboro. This act was an open admission of a romantic relationship. As to be expected, tongues wagged and eyes widened at the sight. By nightfall, it was the talk of the county. Assuming that David and Nancy Yates knew and approved of their daughters' conduct, an angry group of citizens marched to the Yates' farm, threw large rocks through the front windows, expressing their disapproval of what they had witnessed earlier that same day.

With David Yates coming out of his house onto the front porch, someone hollered, "You can't be letting your daughters take up with those Bunker boys!" "It ain't natural."

Another person shouted, "God will strike you dead!"

Some of the leaders of the area talked with David Yates. They were refusing to believe that Yates was not actually encouraging his daughters. They even threatened to burn his crops if he did not promise to control his daughters and see to it that the friendship with Eng and Chang was brought to a close. It became clear that Yates did not know that the sisters had agreed to marry the twins. His wife did not know either. When David returned to the inside of the house, being very confused, he informed his two daughters that any romance with the Bunker boys was over.

Adelaide and Sallie were ready for their parents, and they quickly proclaimed their feelings for Eng and Chang.

David Yates thought that the ruin of his crops and the loss of his livelihood was an excessive price to pay for his daughters' happiness, and tried to persuade the girls to see reason. He pointed out to them that an association of this kind could have no possible future for them and that the whole thing was best to be forgotten. The objection to the twins did not come because of character or social position because the twins carried a 'spotless' reputation. The prejudice was against the race and nationality of the twins. David Yates did not want his daughters to enter an interracial marriage. The fact that the twins were conjoined seemed to be of no concern at all to Mr. Yates.

The twins even went so far as to have a clergyman, Reverend Colby Sparks, visit the Yates' farm to try to convince David Yates that perhaps he had been too hasty. He listened, but he did not change his mind.

As for the twins, they were told quite firmly that while the local people were happy to have them living among them, they were expected to maintain certain standards; in matters of the heart, they must 'keep themselves to themselves,' and no attempts to secure the affections of local girls could be tolerated by the community as a whole.

Since the twins were now banned from the Yates' residence, where their loved ones were being kept as prisoners, Eng and Chang returned to their Traphill house to 'brood' over the injustice of their human condition. Mother Nature had been cruel to the twins and they thought they had finally found a place on earth where they might be treated as normal beings. After all, they had found two women who were willing to help them live and feel as most other men had lived and felt.

Then, when things seemed to be at the darkest hour, a great surprise came to the twins. A note arrived from Adelaide and Sallie asking for a secret meeting on a certain date at a designated place where they would not be seen. Eng and Chang were absolutely beyond disbelief. They had not realized the determination, the aggressiveness, and the independence of the Yates sisters. In just a few days, the secret meeting was held. And, there were more meetings to be held between the two couples. After some months of these secret meetings, this revival of their courtship led to one ultimate decision, they would get married without permission.

There would be lots of speculations in the years to follow as to why the sisters wanted to marry these twins. Some would think that the sisters were rebelling against the strictness of their parents, others would say they just wanted to marry some famous people, still others would say that the girls were marrying for money. But, nobody ever mentioned the fact that they girls were marrying for love.

Just as soon as the decision had been made to get married, Eng and Chang were having second thoughts. They believed the objection of the parents to the wedding was based not only on racial prejudice but also on the idea that each sister would have to live with two men at once. The twins finally came up with one solution, and that was to be surgically separated. If the surgery was successful then the twins could be two separate men for the brides-to-be.

Sarah and Adelaide were both very young, being twenty and nineteen respectively. Definitely, they were not at the age where they would have accepted anybody rather than to remain single. It seemed that the sisters were really in love with the twins and that marriage was the next logical step.

Soon Eng and Chang left Traphill and headed north for Philadelphia to a College of Surgeons, where they met with physicians who had examined them before to determine if they might be separated. At first the doctors refused 'point blank' even to consider an operation, but upon hearing their story of a future marriage, and seeing that the twins were very sincere in something being done, the physicians agreed that they would attempt to separate the twins who were warned that the risk to one or both of them might be death.

Eng and Chang were very adamant in wanting to be separated and were willing to take any and all risks to achieve this separation. They felt that they had little to lose if things did not go well. On the other hand, they thought that years of marriage spent together seemed absolutely impossible.

The arrangements were made and the twins arrived in Philadelphia trying to push to the back of their minds that this surgery might result in being the end of their lives. The doctors were busily making preparations for the operation, and Eng and Chang were waiting, when to the amazement of everybody concerned, Adelaide and Sallie Yates arrived on the scene. The sisters had learned of their plan, possibly from Charles Harris, in whom the twins may have possibly confided. They had followed Eng and Chang to Philadelphia to beg and plead with them to not go through with the surgery. They knew the risk of surgery and they would not allow it. Adelaide and Sallie were almost out of their minds with worry at what the twins were planning to do. They begged the twins to give up the idea. They became hysterical and wept, reassuring the twins that they loved them as they were, and that the four of them could find happiness without the necessity of risking death. At last, Eng and Chang were deeply moved by both the concern and love of Adelaide and Sallie, so they complied with their wishes. The surgery was canceled and the foursome left Philadelphia and returned to Traphill.

Soon after their return to Traphill, Adelaide and Sallie pleaded with David and Nancy Yates for their consent to marry the twins. David and Nancy would not yield. Finally, Adelaide and Sallie went back to the twins to tell them that their parents would not agree to the marriage. Eventually the four of them finally reached a unanimous agreement that they would just take matters into their own hands. They would just elope.

The elopement never happened. The parents finally realized that the daughters intended to marry and could not be dissuaded from their purpose, so the parents allowed them to be married at home. Immediate plans were made for the wedding.

As Irving Wallace stated in the book, The Two, the first formality the twins had to attend to was to obtain the marriage licenses. The licenses were issued, and Eng's read:

STATE OF NORTH CAROLINA
Wilkes County

To any regular minister of the Gospel having the care of souls, of whatever denomination, or to any Justice of the Peace, for said county;

You are hereby licensed and authorized, to solemnize the rites of matrimony between Eng Bunker and Sarah Yates, and join them together as man and wife.

Witness Wm. M. Mastin, Clerk of the County Court, at office in Wilkesboro, the 10th day of April, A.D. 1843, and in the 67th of our independence.

Wm. M. Mastin, c.c.c.

On the same date, Chang received an identical license to wed Adelaide Yates.

The next formality, undertaken three days later, was fulfilling the legal requirement for a marriage bond.

In that period—and in fact until 1868—North Carolina had an "Act Concerning Marriages" that required the posting of a marriage bond before a couple could be legally married. The marriage bond was a guarantee that there was no legal obstacle to the proposed marriage. For example, bigamy was illegal. If either Adelaide or Sallie was committing bigamy (which they were not) by marrying joined brothers, the marriage bond of $1,000 guaranteed by a volunteer bondsman and the grooms would be forfeited. Again, if it was later learned that a free white had married a person of Indian, Negro, or mulatto blood down to the third generation, the marriage would be illegal and the marriage bond forfeited. As it happened, Eng and Chang were Chinese and North Carolina had never passed legislation against Orientals.

Jesse Yates, a brother of Sallie and Adelaide was the volunteer bondsman, and his guarantee of the $1,000 marriage bonds was shared by the twins. There were two identical marriage bonds, one for Chang and one for Eng. Chang's marriage bond read:

CHANG :: ADELAIDE
STATE OF NORTH CAROLINA
Wilkes County

Know all men by these presents that we Chang one of the Siamese Twins and Jesse Yeats (sic) are held and firmly bound unto the state of North Carolina in the sum of one thousand Dollars, current money, to be paid to the said state of North Carolina for the payment whereof, well and truly to be made and done we bind ourselves our Heirs executors and administrators jointly and severally, firmly by these presents sealed with our seal and dated this 13th day of April A.D. 1843.

The condition of the above obligation is such, that the above bounden Chang one of the Siamese Twins has made application for a license for marriage to be celebrated between him and Adelaide Yates of the County aforesaid now in case it should not hereafter appear that there is any lawful cause or impediment in obstruct said marriage, then the above obligation is to be void otherwise to remain in full force and virtue.

CHANG
Jesse Yates

The same day that the marriage bonds were secured, April 13, 1843, the wedding—actually two weddings—took place. These ceremonies took place in the living room of David and Nancy Yates living room mainly because Nancy, weighing over 500 pounds at the time, could not travel over the road to the church where the sisters wanted to be married.

The marriages were performed by the Reverend Colby Sparks, a parson of the local Baptist Church, before a small gathering of family and friends. First, Eng and Sallie were married. Then, Chang and Adelaide were married.

A wedding supper followed with a big dance. At last, the celebration was over and the four newlyweds headed for the Traphill house to start their honeymoon and their domestic life together. In the bedroom of the Traphill house there awaited a "double, double bed" built especially to accommodate all four of them. To the wedding participants, the *Carolina Watchman* newspaper directed a humorous wish: "May the connection be as happy as it will be close!"

The New Foursome

The date was Thursday, April 13, 1843...

The wedding of Eng and Sallie and Chang and Adelaide had now taken place, and the "quartet" of newlyweds was at the Traphill house for the beginning of their honeymoon.

The news of the foursome marriage was reported in newspapers in several countries where the twins were known as performers. Even though the twins were used to receiving publicity, the sisters were not. At least one paper reported that "Both are strong and healthy women," which was probably going to be necessary for such a marriage. There seemed to be a general attitude of surprise that the twins had not chosen circus freaks with whom to share their lives.

In Wilkes County alone there were many people who thought that both of the Bunker marriages were doomed to failure. There were even friendly wagers exchanged as to just how long the brides would endure the situation, especially the special moments of a man and a woman sharing a bed together. How could there ever be any children to come from such an arrangement?

Within three to four weeks after they were married, Eng and Sallie conceived their first child. Also, about four weeks after the marriage, Chang and Adelaide followed by conceiving their first child. Nine months later, on February 10, 1844, Sallie delivered the first of the Bunker children.

She delivered a daughter named Katherine Marcellus. She was named after an early friend of the twins who lived in New York. Then on February 16, only six days later, Chang and Adelaide became the parents of Josephine Virginia.

Katherine Marcellus, first born of Eng and Josephine Virginia, first born of Chang

On March 31, 1845, Sarah gave birth again. This time she gave birth to a daughter, Julia Ann. And only eight days later, Adelaide gave birth to a son, Christopher Wrenn.

With the continuous arrival of new babies fathered by the twins, it was very apparent that they shared very active sexual drives. It seems that almost everyone immediately asked "How did they . . .?" The most typical answer came from a grandson... "Just like everyone else does."

If two's company and three's a crowd, then what would one call four? A convention? Very quickly it became obvious that the house in Traphill was not large enough for two married couples and their growing family of children. So the search began for a larger house. In the summer of 1845, the twins went to look at a farm for sale in Surry County, near the small village of Mount Airy, in what is referred today as the White Plains community. Immediately, they purchased the farm and moved in.

Immediately the twins were very interested in finding a new doctor to look after their children, their wives, and themselves. They were very fortunate in finding two doctors, Dr. Joseph Hollingsworth and Dr. William Hollingsworth. These doctors were brothers, and owned homes and 'consulting rooms' side by side on Main Street in Mount Airy. The twins addressed the physicians as Dr. Joe and Dr. Billy. They became not only patients, but lifelong friends.

Besides devoting their time to the producing and the care of their children, Eng and Chang pursued their careers by utilizing a major asset they had recently purchased. That was their land. With the help of their slaves, they cleared the land of brush and stones, fertilized, plowed, and planted crops. They were even among the first farmers in North Carolina to produce "bright leaf" tobacco, which was very much in demand for cigarettes. They even owned a tobacco press, which was used to manufacture 'plug' chewing tobacco. Eng and Chang taught their slaves how to use this press, and the twins sold a considerable amount of chewing tobacco. Both Eng and Chang liked to smoke pipes, and were fond of chewing tobacco themselves. It seemed that when one got himself a fresh chew, the other did likewise.

The Bunker farm provided most of the food products from the families. They raised milk cows, beef, pigs, sheep, and chickens. They raised corn, wheat, rye, oats, peas, beans, and potatoes. They made butter from their cream, obtained fruit from their orchards, and even kept bees for honey. Like most folk of that era, they were self sufficient in living off the land. And, with their very growing families, they had to do this out of necessity.

Although the twins had minimal formal education, they had a very legible handwriting, liked to read, and kept up with current events. They also enjoyed reading and learning all they could about modern farming. They understood the soil and knew that the biggest and best crops were a result of how the land was kept.

They, like many of their Southern affluent neighbors, owned many slaves to work their land, possibly up to 28 at one time between the two of them. They maintained both "house slaves" and "field slaves." They kept close watch over the work of the slaves, and they were strict taskmasters. They did not want their slaves to become lazy.

The "house slaves," of course worked with household chores, such as cooking, washing clothes, sewing, caring for children, etc. They were under the constant surveillance of their white masters. One of the "house slaves" was Grace Gates, who was given to Sarah and Adelaide as a wedding gift. She was known as "Aunt Grace," and she managed both twins' large broods, all of the Bunker children. Probably, she, like most typical "house slaves," had as much or more influence over the children in her care than their actual mothers. She would nurse the children, rock them to sleep, tell them bedtime stories, punish them and love them. She is reported to have lived to the age of 121 and stayed with the Bunker family until her death. She is reportedly buried in a slave cemetery located on the Bunker farm.

The "field slaves" were to rise before dawn, and they were responsible for feeding the animals and being in the fields ready to work before sunrise. Depending upon the season, these slaves would work the fields, plant or harvest the crops, cut down trees, build fences, and complete other chores that were necessary on the farm.

This writer found it to be rather interesting that Eng and Chang would buy male slaves as young as 8 years old. They would keep them and work them until they were in their early 20's. They made it a practice to never keep a male slave after he reached the age of 25. However, there may have been exceptions to this. The twins thought that by then the male slaves were of the mindset of trying to escape or rebel against their owners. So by this age, the male slaves would be sold or traded for young slaves to carry on the work. The situation was totally different with the female slaves. Both Eng and Chang had an older female slave who may have been thirty-five to forty years old. This older black female was a very important figure in slave culture. She was the one who normally could maintain 'law and order' of the other slaves. She typically maintained influence over the attitudes and work ethics of all of the other slaves on the farm.

Without a doubt, the slaves on the Bunker farm must have found it to be very strange, to not only have masters who were Oriental, but also to have masters who were joined together.

A reporter from the *Southerner*, a publication from Richmond, Virginia once reported the following:

The twins frequently took their slaves out with them on early morning possum-hunting expeditions, and this was one of their favorite recreations.

They attended the local shooting matches, where a turkey or beef was the reward for the best marksman, and Chang and Eng acquired reputations as 'crack shots' with rifles or pistols. It was the object of much curious speculation on the neighbors' part how two men tied together could be so adept, often more adept than a single man.

The farmers in Surry County were frequently plagued by wolves, who wreaked havoc among their livestock. There existed one particularly notorious wolf, christened "Bob-Tail," because he had lost part of his tail in a trap rendered himself the terror of the country by the audacity of his ravages during three successive seasons. All attempts to trap him were totally useless, after the adventure which resulted in depriving him of his caudal extremity, and although frequently seen, no one was ever lucky enough to get a successful shot at him. In truth, there were those who thought he must be the evil one himself, or at least one of his imps, from the apparent impossibility of destroying him. Hundreds had seen him, indeed he was a very Dick Turpin of wolves in his boldness; there was no one who had heard of him, and yet he ranged the country year after year, slaying sheep, swine, and calves with complete impunity. Even darker crimes were attributed to this dreaded animal. A Negro baby was suddenly missed, and nothing was heard from it for several weeks, when portions of its clothing were found in the woods, under such circumstances a showing beyond a doubt that the child had furnished a supper to the wolves. "Bob-tail" had been seen in the vicinity previously, and not a man, woman, or child, doubted but he was the guilty wretch who had accomplished the horrible deed. If he had not been seen, the result would have been the same. His character was so notoriously villainous, that he would certainly have obtained the credit of the transaction.

About the middle of one dark night, the twins were aroused from their slumbers by a noise among their stock. Conjecturing at once that a wolf must be at the bottom of the trouble, they seized a gun, and accompanied by a Negro, hastened out to interfere in the matter. The Negro was provided with a lantern, which he wrapped in his coat for concealment, and the whole part proceeded with great caution towards the scene of disturbance, whereon suddenly bringing the lantern into use, they discovered that this was no other than the redoubtable "Bob-tail," and the next instant the bold intruder lay sweltering in his blood. Of course, Chang and Eng gained considerably in the estimation of their neighbors by this achievement, especially as no more Negro babies were ever known to be stolen and eaten—a convincing proof that "Bob-tail" was the offender in the instance just related.

This writer has in his possession a copy of "Bill of Sale" for Negro slaves existing between Eng and Chang Bunker. This is recorded in the Register of Deeds Office, Dobson, in Surry County, North Carolina.

It reads as follows.

Whereas a co-partnership has heretofore existed between Eng and Chang bunker in the following negro slaves to wig: Berny, a man, age about 60 years; Jean, a Girl, aged about 30 years; Daniel, a Boy, aged about 12 years; (?), a Girl, about 16 years; Thurman, a Boy, aged about 12 years; Moses, a Boy, aged about 12 years; Perry, a Boy, aged about 9 years; Allen or Carey, a Girl, aged about 8 years; Caroline a Girl, aged about 6 years. And whereas it is mutually agreed by and between both parties that the said Chang Bunker is to have the full and entire interest in said Negro slaves. This indenture therefore witnesseth that the said Eng Bunker for and in consideration of the sum of One Dollar to have in hand paid by the said Chang Bunker the receipt whereof is (?) fully acknowledged hath sold and delivered to the said Chang Bunker and his heirs and assigns forever the undersigned one half of the aforesaid slaves. In testimony whereof the said Eng Bunker hath hereto set his hand and seal this 20th day of November AD 1855.

Eng Bunker (seal)
Test. Job Worth, William Rawley

Planning for the Future

The years were 1849 to1861...

Through the years the Bunker families continued to grow. Soon, the money coming in from their crops was not enough to meet the needs of each family. Also, the twins were beginning to realize that their current income would not provide for their children's education.

Still, there was always one avenue open for them to make more money; that was to come out of retirement and return to the "freak show" circuit. Since the twins had been use to being just "homebodies," this decision was going to be a very difficult one. They had become quite accustomed to being away from public life, and they loved being in North Carolina.

In 1849, their old friend, Dr. Edmund H. Doty, visited the twins and suggested that they exhibit themselves again under his management. Eng and Chang considered the thought, even though they had no desire to leave their homes and families and return to exhibiting. Dr. Doty suggest showing the twins, with two of their daughters, Katherine and Josephine, each being age five— for eight months.

The twins finally agreed to the following terms. They were to be paid an annual salary of $8,000, which would be paid to Eng and Chang on a monthly basis. Also, all expenses would be covered by Dr. Doty, and they would not travel at night except by train or boat. Additionally, their work day would only be six hours, and they would be furnished first-class accommodations.

On April 25, 1849, Eng and Chang found themselves back in New York City with two of their children. Surely they remembered the days when they had first come to America some twenty years earlier. Now the Bunker twins were nearing 40; they had wives, children, property, and many responsibilities.

Katherine Marcellus, Eng, Josephine Virginia, Chang

Dr. Doty booked the twins into theaters and auditoriums. However, the series of exhibitions proved to be unsuccessful. Either Dr. Doty's management was poor, or the twins had been overly exhibited in this city. A new curiosity was now being exhibited in New York. This was Tom Thumb, the 25-inch tall midget. He was a new curiosity to the people of the city compared with Eng and Chang whom so many had seen previously.

After spending just six weeks in New York, the twins and their daughters returned to their home in North Carolina with nothing to show for their trouble except an IOU from Dr. Doty, who paid them a third of the amount due many years later.

Meanwhile the twins had received word of their mother's death in Siam. This news cast a big shadow of disappointment on Eng and Chang. For many years they had planned to return to their home to visit their mother, but there was always some reason for the twins not to be able to go.

In April, 1853, a Mr. Howe approached the twins with another offer to do a tour. Even though Eng and Chang were remembering the disappointments from the previous tour, they accepted Mr. Howe's offer. This time they were to be paid weekly. They would be a traveling exhibit, visiting cities and towns along the eastern coastline, heading north into Canada. The twins agreed, provided they could take a child with them. Howe agreed. This time Eng picked the same daughter, Katherine, and Chang picked his son, Christopher, his oldest son.

For the next twelve months Eng and Chang were on the road, traveling more than 4600 miles by boat and coach. Eng and Chang were old traveling hands, but for Katherine and Christopher, it was a most memorable adventure. Both youngsters enjoyed the stage with their fathers where they could dance and even sing a few songs.

Where the foursome traveled, they were constantly hoping to find letters at the next town awaiting them. They were always anxious to hear from their families from back in North Carolina.

A very rare letter exists from this trip, written by Chang and Eng themselves to their wives and children. It is rare because it is one of only a few letters that was actually written by the twins rather than being dictated to someone else who actually wrote the letter.

The letter was written November 29, 1853.

Dear Wives & Children

We have received your (letter of the 22—this day & glad to fine you all well—We got here last Sunday night week—Mr. Howes say he want us to stay here till news year . . . . Catherine & Chris have had very bad cold—but quiet well now & fat—Great many (of) our old friends has come to see us they all say they would like to see all our families together not only friends but the visitor also. We are glad Mr. Coud has call on you—Please tell Mr. Gilmer we shall write to him shortly you may tell him that if he cannot get the corn 25 cents per bushel not to buy at all . . . . We and children want to Mr. Hale last Sunday & took dinner their house. Our house next Mr. Bray—we wanted rent out again just tell Mr. Gilmer to have it rented for the best term he cannot less than $25. We wanted you to tell Mr. Gilmer if any money come to us from Bound tell to put in Mr. G. Handerson of Philad we shall call for it let us know—Our master Mr. Howes take in last week not less than $3000—but his experience are very high say from 2 to 225 dollars a day—Beside he has 5 or 6 different show—they all bring in money—We think none bring so much money as the Siamese Twins & their children.

Good night 12 o'clock
All well your as ever
C & E Bunker

Finally, in April, 1854, they headed home, and this time they were somewhat richer than after their previous adventure. While their financial pressures had eased somewhat, there had remained another pressure that continued to grow more and more nerve-racking. This was the living conditions of both families in the same household. By the summer of 1852, Eng and Sallie had had their sixth child and Chang and Adelaide their fifth. There were now fifteen members in the household plus the house servants. To say the least, things were beginning to become a bit crowded. The Bunker families had become entirely too large to live within the space that was in their present farmhouse. First of all, two wives under one roof may have been one too many. The very thought of both of the wives having to be in the kitchen together, at the dining table and their living room together, and still share their husbands in their 'double' double bed with no privacy whatsoever, was just cause for much bickering and resentment to develop between the sisters. This continued for a number of years before the twins were realizing that something drastic had be done and it needed to be done soon.

In 1852, an experimental separation had been instigated. Adelaide moved into a house in Mount Airy, while Sarah remained on the farm. Then, after three years, Sarah also moved her children into a different house in Mount Airy. But neither of them was happy with their situation.

By 1857 the twins realized something different and drastic had to be done. The four Bunkers had discussed their strange living conditions many times trying to determine a permanent solution that each could accept and be comfortable with. Finally, it was decided that each family should have a separate house and it be located on each family's own farm.

After this decision had been made, the BIG decision was yet to come. And that was in deciding on how the property should be divided. After all, for many years everything—house, land, slaves, animals, etc.—had been 'common' property and owned by both families. And there had been no ill feelings between the twins themselves. So to be assured that decisions were being handled fairly, Eng and Chang decided that an arbitrator was needed to handle the division. Because of the way the real estate was located, the land was not divided equally. Chang received the most valuable part of the farm. In order to equalize the deficiency in value of land, most of the slaves were given to Eng. Eng was never satisfied with the division, but he did not complain of the decision made from the arbitrators.

This is the first home of Eng and Chang along with their families when they first moved from Traphill to White Plains. After the farm was divided this became the home of Eng and Sarah.

Eng retained the original house which they had built when they first moved from Traphill. They made improvements to it.

Very soon after this division of property, Eng and Chang went to work building a house for Chang and his family. This house was located about one mile away from Eng's house.

Once the property had been divided and a second house had been built, there was still another major decision for the Bunker family to make. And, that was, "How would each husband be able to spend time with his wife and family?" They decided that they would spend three days at one brother's house, and then three days at the alternating residences at the end of every third day. For three days Eng and Chang would live in Eng's house with his wife Sarah and their children, leaving Adelaide alone with her children at her house. Then at the end of the third day, Eng and Chang would go over to Chang's house in their horse and carriage and spend three days with Adelaide and their children, leaving Sarah alone with her children at her house.

Home of Chang & Adelaide Bunker. Located about one mile from the home of Eng and Sarah.

75

This arrangement was begun at the very moment that Chang's house was completed. And, this arrangement was continued for the remainder of the twins' lives without exception. There was even an occasion when a child of the twin at whose house they were staying died suddenly. As it happened, the death occurred on the last day of their visit. Since that evening was the scheduled time for the three day visit to end, the twins did leave and move to the home of the other, leaving behind the wife who had to tend the funeral alone, as well as care for the other children.

Another agreement was that each twin was to be the absolute master of his own home. Whatever the host twin did, the joined twin had to agree by keeping silent. They even agreed that neither twin would be allowed to discuss his personal business with anyone while he was residing at his brother's house. He had to wait until the end of the three-day period to return to his own home to discuss the issue.

An old unidentified local newspaper clipping found in another descendant's scrapbook described the pact: "When Eng would enter the house of Chang, he would maintain steadfast silence until the three days had elapsed and he returned to his own house. It was as if he did not exist. He said nothing, did nothing save eat and sleep, saw nothing and was nothing. When the time was done Chang entered upon the role of self-effacement and went with Eng to the latter's house. In his active time Eng lived actively, and transacted all of his business. In his quiescent time he was as if he was not."

This partial separation helped relieve some pressures, but it created an unforeseen disparity that would permanently alter the two families' fortunes. When they divided their property, Chang received the lion's share of the land. In return, Eng kept more slaves. Although Eng wasn't especially happy with the arrangement, his assets actually exceeded Chang's $16,000 by some $3,000. This was at a time when a slave could be bought for $600.

By 1860, with two houses and two farms to support, and a continuous arrival of more children, Eng and Chang realized that their finances were slowly dwindling. They would labor for hours trying to figure out how to save money. But there was little they could do when a crop failed or another baby arrived. So without hesitations, they felt that they had no choice but to return to the show business circuit once again. They made the decision to return to New York to exhibit at the Barnum's American Museum again. This proved to be a financial success as many world celebrities and rulers visited the museum. Mr. P. T. Barnum wanted them to start touring with the circus, but Eng and Chang wanted no part of this. The offer to travel reminded the twins too much of their travels with the Coffins, who wanted every penny they could make from exhibiting the twins.

It seemed that Eng and Chang already had plans even though they had not really announced them. Eng and Chang had seen a large portion of this country, but they had never traveled to the Far West. It was as if California was calling for them, and they wanted to go. It appeared that the right time had come for a return trip to Siam. And, the trip to California would provide a very convenient departure point. Once a definite decision had been made to go to California, the biggest decision confronting the twins was how they would get there, what means of travel would they use? Would they travel by ship, by train, or a combination of both means of travel? Eventually Eng, Chang, and two of Eng's sons, Montgomery and Patrick, boarded a paddle-wheel streamer called The *Northern Light,* in New York Harbor and headed south. It was an eight-day journey to Panama, where the Bunker's then rode a wood burning train that took them the short distance from the Atlantic to the Pacific side. Then for 16 more days, they rode the steamer *Uncle Sam* to San Francisco, arriving there on December 6, 1860.

At last Eng and Chang were in San Francisco, in a new city that had never seen them, hoping to replenish their 'purses' before continuing on to their reunion with their older brother in Siam. There was a great deal of publicity generated for the twins, and they were very successful with their exhibiting. However, circumstances did arise causing the twins to change their plans of returning to Siam. A local newspaper in San Francisco published an article that was going to be a life changing event for Eng and Chang. In that article, it seemed that Abraham Lincoln was seemingly winning the presidency. Many of the leaders of the South had declared that their states would leave the Union if Lincoln was elected. Actually, the big question of slavery was on the minds of many of the citizens. With most of the people in the North being against slavery, Eng and Chang had always relied on their slaves to run their farms for them. What would happen in they had to give up their slaves? There was absolutely nothing that the twins could do about their problems while they were in California. They did decide to cancel all plans for going to Siam. Then they would have to return to their homes in North Carolina.

In the next few weeks Eng and Chang traveled into various cities and towns throughout California. People came out in large numbers to see them and the newspapers gave them very kind reviews. One writer even wrote that the twins ". . . were accompanied by two sons—boys, of nine and twelve years old—bright and intelligent boys."

On February 11, 1861, Eng, Chang and Eng's sons, boarded the paddle-wheel steamer *Golden Age* for the beginning of their voyage back to North Carolina. As they moved through the Golden Gate strait leaving San Francisco, they did share great feelings that their two-month journey into the west had been both fascinating and financially successful. But as they were facing the open sea, they could feel apprehension, not only for their future, but also for the future of their country.

Just about the time that Eng and Chang began their journey back to North Carolina from California, the United States seemed to begin to fall apart. South Carolina had threatened to leave the Union if a Republican were elected President. And, Republican Abraham Lincoln did win the presidency on November 6, 1860. On December 20, the Convention of the People of South Carolina had unanimously voted to secede from the Union. Other Southern states were following quickly. Then by the first week in February, the confederate States of America was formed. The terrible United States divide had begun.

Finally, Eng and Chang arrived back home in Mount Airy, North Carolina after 26 days of ocean voyages and traveling home from New York. They had about a month to reacquaint themselves with their families and organize their business affairs before the last peace that they would know for four years would come to an abrupt end.

On April 12, 1861, confederate guns fired on Fort Sumter, South Carolina, which was federal property. Following 34 hours of bombardment, Fort Sumter fell. A week later, President Lincoln ordered a blockade of all Southern port cities. Men were called up to fight. North Carolina was the eleventh state to secede from the Union on May 20 when it joined the Confederate States of America. The Civil War had begun.

The 21 Children

First of all, this writer found it to be very interesting that there was a definite pattern in the order of the birth of the children of Eng and Sarah Bunker and Chang and Adelaide Bunker. Eng and Sarah always had a child, followed just a few days later by Chang and Alelaide having a child. The birth orders of the children will be listed first. I will use **E&S** for the children of Eng and Sarah. I will use **C&A** for the children of Chang and Adelaide.

E&S   Katherine Marcellus, b. February 10, 1844.
C&A   Josephine Virginia Bunker, b. February 16, 1844.

E&S   Julia Ann Bunker, b. March 31, 1845.
C&A   Christopher Wren Bunker, b. April 08, 1845.

E&S   Steven Decatur, b. March 12, 1846.
C&A   Nancy Adelaide Bunker, b. June 05, 1847.

E&S   James Montgomery, b. December, 16,, 1848.
C&A   Susan Mariana Bunker, b. October 10, 1849.

E&S   Patrick Henry Bunker, b. May 7, 1850.
C&A   *no record of a child being born in this order.*

E&C Rosalyn Etta Bunker, b. January 28, 1852.
C&A Victoria Bunker, b. May 25, 1852.

E&C William Oliver Bunker, b. January 31, 1855.
C&A Louisa Emaline Bunker, b. April 13, 1855

E&C Frederick Marshall Bunker, b. February 1, 1857.
C&A Albert Lemuel Bunker, b. April 22, 1857.

E&S Rosella Virginia Bunker, b. 1859.
C&A Jesse Lafayette Bunker, b. April 07, 1861.

E&S Georgianna Columbia Bunker, b. May 09,1863.
C&A Margaret Elizabeth Bunker, b. October 06, 1863.

E&S Robert Edward Bunker, b. April 17, 1865.
C&A Hattie Irene Bunker, b. September 12, 1868.

Katherine Marcellus "Kate" Bunker

Katherine or "Kate" was the first-born child of Eng and Sarah Yates Bunker. She was born February 10, 1844, in Traphill, Wilkes County, NC. She was named after Miss Catherine Bunker of New York, an early friend of the twins.

In, 1868, Eng's oldest daughter, Kate, brilliant young lady with a well cultivated mind, had been for some time growing more and more delicate in health, and it was greatly feared by her family and acquaintances that she was falling prey to a fatal malady.

It was hoped that perhaps a voyage across the salt sea might prove beneficial or that some physicians of London or Edinburg might be advantageous. She was anxious to go. Kate was twenty four and Chang's daughter, Nancy Adelaide "Nannie," age twenty one, went on this trip, leaving December 5, 1868. Both daughters kept written records of their trip. Many passengers became sick on the trip – fourteen days at sea.

Kate was seen by physicians on the staff of the Edinburg Medical Center. Her diagnosis was pulmonary consumption, far advanced.

The twins arranged to meet with Sir James Young Simpson, the renowned Scottish physician who was professor of medicine at Edinburgh University, to consult his opinion as regarding the propriety of a surgical operation to separate them. The physician apparently could do nothing to improve Kate's state of health. Neither did he think the Siamese Twins could successfully be separated. By August 5, 1869, they were safely home in Mount Airy, NC.

Katherine "Kate" Marcellus Bunker died in 1871 at age 27 of consumption, or what we know today as tuberculosis. (This bio was copied from findagrave.com) There are no records available to indicate where Kate Bunker was buried. According to a May 12, 2002 survey of White Plains Baptist Church Cemetery, Surry County, North Carolina, Katherine Marcellus Bunker is not listed as having been buried in this cemetery. It is believed that she may have been buried elsewhere on Bunker property, possibly where her mother, Sarah Yates Bunker, is buried.

Josephine Virginia Bunker

Josephine Virginia was the first-born child of Chang and Adelaide Yates Bunker. She was born February 14, 1844, in Traphill, Wilkes County, NC. She died, August 16, 1867. There are no records available to indicate where Josephine Virginia Bunker is buried. According to a May 12, 2002 survey of White Plains Baptist Church Cemetery, Surry County, North Carolina, Josephine Virginia Bunker is not listed as having been buried in this cemetery.

Josephine Virginia was the only one of Chang's ten children to die while Chang was still alive. She was, of course, the first child and a favorite daughter. She suffered a heart attack while riding home on her horse and fell to the ground dead.

Julia Ann Bunker

Julia Ann Bunker was the second daughter of Eng and Sarah Yates Bunker. She was born March 31, 1845 in Traphill, Wilkes County, North Carolina. She died February 27, 1865, at age 19, (the same year as her sister Georgiana died) in Surry County, North Carolina. The cause of death is unknown. There are no records available to indicate where Julia Ann Bunker was buried. According to a May 12, 2002 survey of White Plains Baptist Church Cemetery, Surry County, North Carolina, Julia Ann Bunker is not listed as having been buried in this cemetery.

Christopher Wren Bunker

Christopher Wren Bunker was the first son and second child of Chang and Adelaide Yates Bunker. He was born April 8, 1845, in Traphill, Wilkes County, North Carolina. He died April 2, 1932, and is buried at the Antioch Baptist Church Cemetery, Mount Airy, Surry County, North Carolina. He was married to Mary E. Haynes Bunker.

Christopher was a Confederate veteran. He was one of Surry County's most successful farmers.

Their child:
Christopher Lee Bunker, 1883

Christopher was nearly twenty-nine when his father died. As in most families, there seems to be family "squabbles" when there is a death of a parent. Christopher had been the one to keep his father's farm in operation when his father was away for any length of time. Unfortunately, after Chang's death, Christopher became totally separated from his mother Adelaide, and most of his brothers and sisters. This is what happened according to an account given by Irvin Wallace in his book, The Two. Christopher was taken to court in a property dispute. Christopher won the case, but in so doing, incurred $525.15 in costs. He felt, under the terms of Chang's will that this sum was an estate expense, not his alone. Adelaide would not have it. Christopher sued his mother, naming his brothers and sisters as co-defendants. The case was fought in the courts for twenty-six years. In 1905, the North Carolina Supreme Court held for Christopher. He won, but because of an error, he did not collect. In the meantime, the legal action had alienated him from the family.

In 1882, when Christopher was 37, he married, had a son Christopher L., who in turn married an Emma Snow who was also from Mount Airy. Christopher told his son and daughter-in-law that he would will them his 1,000 acre farm if they had children. But, if they did not, the property was to go to the Baptist Children's Homes of North Carolina. Christopher, Sr., died in 1932 at the age of eighty-eight without grandchildren. So as he had promised a large portion of his estate—worth half a million dollars three decades later—went to the Baptists, who used a portion of the inheritance to build Bunker Cottage at the Kennedy Home in Kinston, North Carolina.

Stephen Decatur Bunker

Stephen Decatur Bunker was the first son and third child of Eng and Sarah Yates Bunker. He was born April 12, 1846, in White Plains Community, Surry County, North Carolina. He died March 25, 1920, at age seventy-three. He is buried at the White Plains Baptist Church, Surry County, North Carolina. He was the oldest child Eng left behind at his death. He was left in charge of his father's farm.

Stephen enlisted in the Civil War on July 02, 1864, and while fighting with the 37th Battalion of the Virginia Calvary, CST, near Winchester, he was wounded. In 1865, he was wounded a second time. It has been reported that after Stephen's death, his widow Susan applied for and obtained a Confederate Civil War pension from the state of North Carolina.

He married Susan Alice Nichols Bunker, and was the father of five children:

1. Nettie May Bunker, 1891-1918
2. Buffy Bunker, 1892-1898
3. Stephen Dixon Bunker, 1893-1893
4. Stephen Dana Bunker, 1895-1954
5. Woo Eng Bunker, 1901-1980

Nancy Adelaide Bunker

Nancy Adelaide Bunker was the second daughter and third child of Chang and Adelaide Yates Bunker. She was born June 5, 1847, in White Plains, Surry County, NC. She died February 17, 1874, at the age of 27, of tuberculosis that she had contacted from her ailing cousin Katherine. She died the day before Eng and Chang's autopsy report was read to the College of Physicians in Philadelphia. She never married. She is buried at the

White Plains Baptist Church Cemetery, Surry County, North Carolina.

James Montgomery Bunker

James Montgomery Bunker was the second son and fourth child of Eng and Sarah Yates Bunker. He was born December 15, 1848, in White Plains, Surry County, North Carolina. He died April 24, 1921 in Sumner County, Kansas, where he homesteaded in Milan, Kansas. He is buried At Milan Cemetery, Sumner County, Kansas in the original cemetery, Section 2, Lot 6. He was married 1st in Sumner Co., Kansas, to Cecilia Munro on May 27, 1884. He married 2nd on November 7, 1886 to Anna Laura Mears. James died of heart failure. Funeral services for him were held at home.

His children:
1. Laura Bessie Bunker, 1887 – 1889
2. Wiley Hanible Montgomery Bunker, 1889 – 1950
3. Sally Winston Bunker, 1891 – 1974
4. James Edward Bunker, 1895 – 1964

5. Ethel Bunker Dovel, 1900 – 1976
6. Eng Bunker, 1905 – 1975
7. Ray Bunker, 1908 – 1950

Susan Mariana Bunker

Susan Mariana Bunker was the third daughter and fourth child of Chang and Adelaide Yates Bunker. She was born October 10, 1849 in White Plains, Surry County, North Carolina. She died March 02, 1922, in Sandpoint, Bonner County, Idaho, when she was living with her oldest daughter, Hattie. She was seventy two years old. She married Squire Gordon Jones on November 28, 1877 at Mount Airy, North Carolina.

Their children:
1. Oscar Lee Jones 1878
2. Franklin Davis Jones 1880
3. Hattie Emma Jones 1882
4. Squire Henry Jones 1883
5. Cleveland Boyd Jones 1885

6. Edgar Cecil Jones 1887
7. John Percy Jones 1891
8. Chattie Victoria Jones 1896

Patrick Henry Bunker

Patrick Henry Bunker was the third son and the fifth child of Eng and Sarah Yates Bunker. He was born May 7, 1850, in White Plains, Surry County, North Carolina. After the Civil War, he migrated to Kansas with his brother James. He died May 24, 1938, in Medicine Lodge, Barber County, Kansas. He and a brother went west and bought farms in Summer County, Kansas. The brother died several years earlier.

Patrick married Mary Jane Bradley Miller. He and his wife had three sons and three daughters. Patrick remembers that "One day my wife told me she wanted a divorce. She asked for the custody of the children too." He told her that she did not want to really do that but she insisted. Patrick believed, "no man ever made anything 'lawing' with his wife so I deeded her the farm and everything in it. After a while she married again and I reckon she set the children against me. Anyhow, they never came to see me. I knew where some of them were for a while but I finally lost track."

Their children:
1. James "Henry" Bunker, 1882
2. Delia Lee Bunker, 1885
3. Joseph Ancil Bunker, 1886
4. Phrony Myrtle Bunker, 1887
5. George Patrick Bunker, 1888
6. Nancy Ann Bunker, 1889

Patrick Henry fell on hard times and in his old age became an inmate at the county poor farm in Medicine Lodge. He spent a good share of his time fishing during his stay at the county farm and did a lot of reminiscing about his famous father and his uncle. Patrick Henry was eighty-eight when he died. He is buried in Highland Cemetery, Medicine Lodge, Barber County, Kansas.

Rosalyn Etta Bunker

Rosalyn Etta Bunker was the third daughter and the sixth child of Eng and Sarah Yates Bunker. She was born January 27, 1852, White Plains, Surry County, North Carolina. She died February 14, 1852, of third-degree burns from an open fireplace and was the first child belonging to Eng and Sarah to die. Since the White Plains Baptist Church Cemetery was not established until 1854, it is possible that Rosalyn Etta Bunker may have been buried in what is generally referred to as the 'Slave Cemetery' off

Bunker Road in White Plains, Surry County, North Carolina.

Victoria Bunker

Victoria Bunker was the fourth daughter and the fifth child of Chang and Adelaide Yates Bunker. She was born in White Plains, Surry County, North Carolina, May 25, 1852. She died November 15, 1896, age forty-four. She was first married to Nathaniel "Nat" Bolejack of Stokes County, NC, near Germanton. Her father bought her a farm near Germanton, called the Bunker Farm. She only lived there for only a short time. Her husband left her and her father came and got her and the farm was sold.

Their Children:
1. Ida Virginia Bolejack 1872
2. Allie V. Bolejack 1874

Victoria's second marriage was to Dr. Frank Talifferno. They had a pecan orchard in Oklahoma. He preceded her in death. She is reported to have died at King's Home, Ok, of cancer. Place of burial is unknown.

William Oliver Bunker and wife Judy

William Oliver Bunker was the fourth son and the seventh child of Eng and Sarah Yates Bunker. He was born January 31, 1855, in White Plains, Surry County, North Carolina. He died July 15, 1932, at the age of seventy-seven. He made his home in Mount Airy his entire life. He is buried at White Plains Baptist Church, White Plains, Surry County, North Carolina. His first marriage was to Francis Britt.

Their children:
1. William Francis Bunker, 1878-1898
2. Rosa Virginia Bunker, 1880-1898
3. Annie Lou Bunker, 1882- 1894

His second marriage was to Judy Ross Laffoon.
Their children:
1. Napoleon B. Bunker, 1890

2. Oliver Wendell Bunker, 1892
3. Harden Russell Bunker, 1894
4. Fred Bunker, 1897
5. Otto Garden Bunker, 1898
6. Byron Decatur Bunker, 1900
7. Erie Bunker, 1902
8. Vera Mahaley Bunker, 1904
9. Dennis Nathan Bunker, 1905
10. Julia Ann Bunker, 1908
11. Robert Taylor Bunker, 1910

Robert Taylor Bunker was the 11th and youngest child of William Oliver and Judy Ross Laffoon. He was also the grandson of Eng and Sarah Yates Bunker. Robert married Nellie Mae Key and they were the parents of the first set of twins born in the lineage of Eng and Chang. Wayne "Eng" Bunker and Wade "Chang" Bunker were born on March 03, 1941. They were named in honor of their great grandfather and their great uncle.

It should be noted that William had a grand-daughter, Gladys, who was a nurse and a Lieutenant Commander in the United States Navy. She visited Siam (Thailand) and was received with much royalty because she was related to Eng and Chang.

Louisa Emaline Bunker

Louisa Emaline Bunker was the fifth daughter and the sixth child of Chang and Adelaide Yates Bunker. She was born April 13, 1855, in White Plains, Surry County, North Carolina. Louisa was specifically provided for in her father's will since she was deaf. She died March 30, 1934, in Raleigh, Wake County, North Carolina. She was deaf and was married to Zacharias W. Haynes in 1873. He, too, was deaf because of scarlet fever contracted at age 10. They are buried at Oakwood Cemetery, Raleigh, Wake County, North Carolina.

Their children:
1. Christopher Haynes, 1876
2. Alice Irene Haynes, 1875
3. Edwin Byron Haynes, 1892
4. Carrie Adelaide Haynes, 1879
5. Mabel Louisa Haynes, 1881

6. John Walter Haynes, 1883
7. Effie Haynes, 1886
8. Ernest E. Haynes, 1889
9. Infant, 1891
10. Alfred Milton Haynes, Sr., 1896

Frederick Marshall Bunker

Frederick Marshall Bunker was the fifth son and the eighth child of Eng and Sarah Yates Bunker. He was born February 1, 1857, White Plains, Surry County, North Carolina. He was only 16 when his father died. Then he moved to Missouri and according to a descendant, was killed in a bar-room fight in St. Louis. He died October 23, 1886, and is buried in Argonia Cemetery, Argonia, Sumner County, Kansas. (Plot: Lot 272, Space 1). He was married to Lydia Bunker.

Albert Lemuel Bunker

Albert Lemuel Bunker was the second son and the seventh child of Chang and Adelaide Yates Bunker. He was born April 22, 1857, White Plains, Surry County, North Carolina. He died October 08, 1944, age eighty-seven, and he is buried at the White Plains Baptist Church, White Plains, Surry County, North Carolina. He inherited Chang's house from his mother, Adelaide. He remained a bachelor until the age of sixty-five. He was then married to Nina Angel, who had been a major of music at Meredith Baptist College for Women.

Their children
1. Adelaide Angell Bunker Sink, 1922
2. Dorothy Knoontz Bunker, 1923
3. Nancy Louise Bunker, 1925

Rosella Virginia Bunker and her mother Sarah

Rosella Virginia Bunker was the fourth daughter and the ninth child of Eng and Sarah Yates Bunker. She was born June 01, 1859, White Plains, Surry County, North

Carolina. She was only fourteen when her father died. She married George Whitfield Ashby and was the only daughter of Eng to raise a family. She had a son, George Ashby, who grew up to become president of the Union Pacific Railroad. She died October 09, 1941 and is buried in Oakdale Cemetery, Mount Airy, Surry County, North Carolina.

Their children:
1. Jim Patterson Ashby, 1882
2. Fredrick Byron Ashby, 1884
3. George Franklin Ashby, 1885
4. Annie Mae Ashby, 1888
5. Effie Pearl Ashby, 1892
6. Bryan Haywood Ashby, 1895

Jesse Lafayette Bunker

Jesse Lafayette Bunker was the third son and the eighth child of Chang and Adelaide Yates Bunker. He was born April 07, 1861, White Plains, Surry County, North Carolina. He died June 09, 1909, having been struck by lightning on his farm, and is buried in the Critz Cemetery, Mount Airy, Surry County, North Carolina. This is the small family cemetery that is located on beside Calvary Baptist Church, South Franklin Road, Mount Airy, North Carolina. Jesse was born deaf and mute. He married Emma Davis.

Their children:
1. Fred Murphy Bunker, 1886
2. Burton
3. Arthur

4. Mary Irene Bunker, 1889
5. Davis Bunker

<u>Georgianna Columbia Bunker</u>

Georgianna Columbia Bunker was the fifth daughter and the tenth child of Eng and Sarah Yates Bunker. She was born May 9, 1863 in White Plains, Surry County, North Carolina and died in September, 1865, at age 2 years and five months. She was scalded by hot water and died from the burns. She died the same year as her sister, Julia. She may have been buried in what is generally referred to as the 'Slave Cemetery' off Bunker Road in White Plains, Surry County, North Carolina.

Margaret Elizabeth "Lizzie" Bunker
and husband, Caleb Hill Haynes

Margaret Elizabeth "Lizzie" Bunker was the sixth daughter and the ninth child of Chang and Adelaide Bunker. She was born October 06, 1863, in White Plains, Surry County, North Carolina. She was ten years old when her father died. She died November 03, 1950. She married

Caleb Hill Haynes. She is buried at Oakdale Cemetery, Mount Airy, Surry County, North Carolina, (Section 7, Lot 34, Plot 2).

Their children:
1. Minnie Ruth Haynes, 1890
2. Joseph Bunker Haynes, 1891
3. Grace Adelaide Haynes, 1893
4. Caleb Vance Haynes, 1895*
5. Rachel Elizabeth Haynes, 1897
6. Margaret Lucile Haynes, 1898
7. Ethel Marie Haynes, 1901
8. Charles Haynes, 1903
9. Lester Yates Haynes, 1904
10. Mary Louise Haynes, 1906

The fourth child of Caleb and Lizzie was Caleb Vance Haynes who became a Major General of the United States Air Force. He was also an aide to President Wilson at the Versailles Peace Conference, chief of the American Bomber Command in China during World War II, and recipient of the Silver Star and Distinguished Flying Cross.

Robert Edward "Bob" Bunker

Robert Edward Bunker was the sixth son and the eleventh child of Eng and Sarah Yates Bunker. He became known as Big Bob. He was born April 17, 1865, in White Plains, Surry County, North Carolina. He was only eight years old when his father, Eng, died.

Big Bob died January 25, 1951, at the age of eighty-five in White Plains, Surry County, North Carolina. He died at home, same house, same bed that he was born on, and the same house and same bed that his father, Eng, and Uncle Chang died on. This is stated on his death certificate. He is buried at the White Plains Friends Meeting Cemetery, White Plains, Surry County, North Carolina. He married Fannie Elizabeth Jenkins.

Their children:
1. Katherine Marcellus Bunker, 1899
2. Sallie Ann Bunker, 1901
3. Albert Montgomery Bunker, 1903
4. John Spach Bunker, 1906
5. Charlie Bernard Bunker, 1909
6. Ralph Conoy Bunker, 1911
7. Edward Merritt Bunker, 1913
8. Nancy Adelaide Bunker, 1916
9. Thomas Settle Bunker, 1918
10. Hubert L. Bunker, 1923

Edward Lafayette and Hattie Bunker Patterson

Hattie was the seventh daughter and the tenth child of Chang and Adelaide Yates Bunker. She was born September 12, 1868, White Plains, Surry County, North Carolina. She died November 18, 1945, Toast, Surry County, North Carolina. She married Edward Lafayette Patterson. She is buried at Oakdale Cemetery, Mount Airy, Surry County, North Carolina,

Their children:
1. Lillian Bunker Patterson, 1888
2. Maurice Patterson 1890
3. Adelaide "Bessie" Patterson 1894
4. Virginia "Eizabeth" Patterson 1900
5. Josephine Jessica Patterson, 1902
6. Albert Lafayette Patterson, 1904
7. Jesse Patterson, 1911

There were 4 more babies, 2 were stillborn and 2 died as infants.

The Great War and its Effects

The years were 1861 to 1868...

Eng and Chang arrived back in Mount Airy, North Carolina in early March, 1861. It was a very different place from what they had left approximately four months earlier. Much of the South was bracing for war, and Abraham Lincoln had since been sworn into office as President of the United States. The United States was beginning to break apart. South Carolina, which had threatened to leave the Union if a Republican were elected President. On December 20, the Convention of the People of South Carolina voted to secede from the Union. As a result, many other southern states soon followed. Then in early February, the Confederate States of America was formed. The "great divide" had actually happened.

On April 12, 1861, Confederate guns fired on Fort Sumter, outside of Charleston, South Carolina, which was federal property. After thirty six hours of bombardment, Fort Sumter fell. The Civil War had begun. On April 19, President Lincoln had ordered a blockade of all southern port cities. On May 3, the President called for volunteers to the Union Army. And, on May 6, 1861, the Confederate Congress declared that a state of war existed between the South and the North.

Then on May 20, the one thing that Eng and Chang were dreading most came to pass. On this day, North

Carolina became the eleventh state to secede from the Union, join the Confederacy, and enter the war.

The Thailand natives were living as naturalized citizens in North Carolina when the Union army raided the area and drafted some of the locals to join their army, despite the fact that many of them, including the Bunker brothers, were Confederate supporters. It was once reported that Union General George Stoneman put the names of all men over 18 years of age into a lottery wheel and selected names at random. Eng's name was drawn, but Chang's wasn't. Since the conjoined twins could not be separated, there wasn't much that Stoneman could do. Neither brother ended up fighting in the war, although both of their eldest sons, Christopher Wren Bunker and Stephen Bunker, joined and fought for the Confederacy. Eng and Chang also learned that they would be taxed to raise money to support the newly organized Confederate army. Their wives, along with most of the women in the area, were expected to not only maintain their own families, but also to sew for the soldiers and to nurse if they knew of any wounded soldiers who might need their care.

At the onset of the Civil War, 1860 records in Surry County showed that both Eng and Chang were very comfortable in their financial situations. At the time, Eng had eight children and Chang had seven. By 1862, after a full year of the war, the twins were still financially comfortable. Eng was shown to have 19 slaves and Chang had 11 slaves. By 1863, the twins were continuing to prosper with Eng owning 21 slaves and Chang owning 10 slaves. Then by 1864, the tax summation revealed Eng owning 21 slaves and Chang owning 12 slaves.

Sarah and Adelaide lived under constant stress due to their atypical lifestyles. They shared the stress of each having to live with "her" husband and "his" brother. With the onset of the war, they were under much additional stress, and they became more and more at odds with one another.

On the other hand, the twins were beginning to suffer from the higher taxes imposed to help finance the war. Then, the Confederate treasury minted its own money and sold war bonds to raise cash. Eng and Chang were forced to use the newly issued Confederate money and to buy war bonds. They also loaned their friends and neighbors money to live on. The twins felt a lot of guilt as they watched men their own age go off to battle, leaving their wives and children behind. The least Eng and Chang could do, in their own opinion, was to help their neighbors with financial problems. Of course in the end, the confederate money greatly depreciated in value as the war progressed and the prospects of winning grew rather dim.

Sarah and Adelaide were somewhat exempt from so many of the hardships and inconveniences that other North Carolina women had to undergo, such as farming the fields in the absence of their husbands, the general worrying as to whether or not their husbands were even alive, etc. However, they still worked very hard sewing clothes for the soldiers, preparing food for troops, and caring for the wounded.

On April 1, 1863, the first member of either of the Bunker families, Christopher Wrenn Bunker, the second oldest child of Chang, enlisted in the Confederate Calvary.

Stephen Decatur Bunker, oldest son of Eng and Sarah Bunker, enlisted in 1864

A year later Eng's oldest son, Stephen Decatur Bunker, joined and headed off to war. With Sarah and Adelaide each having a son in battle, they were both becoming more and more increasingly tense. Like so many of their friends, they were afraid of hearing the news that a son had been lost or killed.

Eng and Chang were also sharing the concern of their wives about their sons, but they also were trouble about financial matters. In the beginning of the war, most Southerners believed that the war against the North would be quick, possibly lasting only a couple of months. But as these months turned into years, and the cost of human lives and war machinery was constantly increasing, while the value of Confederate money was rapidly decreasing. Loans that had been made to neighbors were not being repaid.

In August, 1864, Christopher Bunker was wounded and captured by Union soldiers. The news stunned the Bunker families. A month later, Stephen Bunker had also been wounded in battle. So there was a major mood change in the homes of both Eng and Chang.

On the morning of February 5, 1865, a Union lieutenant announced to the Confederate soldiers where Christopher was being held, that "Parole exchange of prisoners has been agreed upon between the United States and the Confederate States!" A month later, on March 4, 1865, Christopher Bunker took the oath of allegiance to the United States and was released. Christopher made his way back home to Mount Airy on April 17, 1865, and for him, the war was over.

As for Stephen Bunker, he was wounded in battle on September 3, 1864. Apparently the wound was not serious because he was back in action very soon. A very short time after Christopher had returned home, Stephen was wounded a second time. This happened just a few days before all fighting had ceased. Stephen was sent home to Mount Airy. The war was officially ended on May 29, 1965, when President Andrew Johnson granted amnesty and pardon to all who had taken part in the "rebellion."

The South was left in shambles. And, so were the financial prospects of Eng and Chang Bunker. One of the twins' major sources of income during the war years had been the interest from loans that they had made. They had not realized that the defeat of the Confederacy would result in a total collapse of its currency.

However, the greatest loss for the twins was really not in the money and interest owed to them, but in their slave holdings. In 1864, according to the tax records of Surry County, Eng owned 21 slaves valued at $17,050. Chang owned 12 slaves worth $9,500.

To this day, some family members contend that Chang knew at the time that Lincoln planned to free the slaves, but this hardly seems plausible. According to at least one biographer, though, Adelaide had pressed for land over slaves during the property division. In any case, the disparity would have far-reaching consequences, since some modern-day descendants of Eng still consider themselves "the poor side" of the family.

In 1866, a year after the war ended, a new tax listing did not make any mention of any slaves owned by either twin. However, Eng was credited with 300 acres of land worth $1,000 while Chang was credited with 425 acres worth $6,000.

With the abolishment of slavery in the South and all slaves being liberated, Eng and Chang were forced to tell all their thirty-three slaves that they were free. The slaves laid aside their hoes and shovels, formed lines, and marched off the farms to enjoy their new-found freedom. Within a few days, one of the former slaves returned to the Bunker farms and requested to resume his old job as a paid employee. In the weeks that followed, most of the other freed slaves returned to the Eng and Chang farms. They had discovered for themselves that they had no place to go, no jobs, no money, and no place to live. They were ready to return to work, but this time for salaries. Eng and Chang hired as many as they were able to support, but the others just drifted away hoping to seek employment at another location. Now that the slaves were paid employees, adding a new expense to the twins' overhead, the financial situation of Eng and Chang was almost in ruins.

Many believed after the war that the twins had been left bankrupt. This was not the case even though they were desperate to provide security to their very large families. They still owned their land, their homes, their furnishings, and were able to at least make a sufficient living from their farms. With the financial situation of so many in the South being desperate, Eng and Chang made the decision in the fall of 1865 that they ". . . engage to travel again . . . ."

There was a Simon Zimmerman, who at one time had been a wealthy railroad investor and a native of Baltimore. Before the Civil War, he had married and moved to North Carolina. Like all others, the war had depleted Mr. Zimmerman of his fortune and plunged him into bankruptcy. This was the person who had the idea of recouping part of his wealth by enticing Eng and Chang back into show business with him as manager.

Eng and Chang were now fifty-four years old when they started this tour throughout the Eastern and Midwestern sections of the United States. The tours lasted for approximately three years. However, there was a problem with managers, and it seems that the twins went through at least three other managers during this period.

The twins were not being very successful at drawing in crowds or at increasing finances under any of the managers. So with one last option of a Judge H. P. Ingalls becoming their manager, things started to improve financially. Judge Ingalls had the brilliant ideal of including photographs of their wives and/or children in their advertisements. This was to remind the public that these joined twins were married to two normal sisters, and that this strange marriage had actually produced offspring. Eng and Chang had no objections to publicizing their wives and to exhibit their children again. Earlier tours, the twins had brought along at least one child each to exhibit with them anyway.

In the spring of 1865, Eng and Chang brought their wives, Sarah and Adelaide, and two of their children, Patrick and Albert to a renowned photographic studio of Mathew Brady located in New York City, for a photograph that would be used for a publicity campaign.

When the Bunker's arrived at the studio, they were ushered into a photography room, seated in a comfortable group with Eng and Chang in the center and their wives, Sarah and Adelaide on either side. Their two sons, Patrick and Albert were seated at their feet. Within minutes the camera shutter snapped, and the official photograph for Eng and Chang to officially join the gallery of immortals was created.

During these exhibitions, Eng and Chang were continuing to draw larger crowds. They were being paid approximately $50.00 per week, a very good source of profit. They had gained enough money by the end of 1868 that Eng was able to buy a very good farm adjoining his home tract, making his total farm as valuable as Chang's.

In the meantime, arrangements had been made for Eng and Chang to meet with P. T. Barnum again. Barnum's New American Museum had burned down and he was struggling to make a comeback. He was planning a double feature of creatures—namely to send Tom Thumb and his new midget wife around the world, and Chang and Eng Bunker to England.

The twins accepted the offer. They were in their late 50's with most of their lives behind them. They had married and fathered children. They had met hundreds of thousands of people—rich, poor, famous, unknown. They had seen many countries, states, and cities around the world. But yet one wish continued to linger with them. They longed to be individuals, separate beings who could walk and sit and lie alone. Sarah and Adelaide wanted this for their husbands. Their children wanted this for their fathers. Mr. P. T. Barnum offered them one final chance to make this wish come true. No doctor in the United States would operate on them. But perhaps there might be someone in England who would perform the surgery. Was it worth the try?

The Last Voyage

The years were 1867 to 1870...

A couple of years prior to 1870 arrangements had been made for Eng and Chang to begin preparing themselves for what would be their final tour. These plans were for Eng and Chang to travel to New York to meet with P. T. Barnum for one last time. Barnum's American Museum had completely burned in recent months and he had been struggling for a way to regain his financial loss. He was planning a double feature of creatures, namely Tom Thumb and his new midget wife would tour around the world while Eng and Chang would tour England.

The twins accepted Mr. Barnum's offer. They were now 57 years old and, of course, most of their lives were behind them. They had married and fathered children. They had traveled and met hundreds of thousands of people, rich, poor, famous, unknown. They had traveled over a large part of the world, large cities and small towns. But yet one wish still was lingering with them. They had longed to be individuals who could walk, sit, and lie alone. Not only did Sarah and Adelaide want this for the twins but also the children. Without being aware of the fact, Mr. P. T. Barnum offered them a final chance to make their wish come true. They had been unsuccessful in finding a doctor in the United States who would separate them. So perhaps there might be someone in England who would. At least it was worth a try.

Mr. Barnum was not aware that Eng and Chang were planning to bring some extra guests on the trip. Kate, Eng's oldest daughter, who was 24 at the time, was suffering from an unknown illness. She was steadily growing weaker. Maybe one of the overseas specialists might be able to help. Also, Nannie, Chang's oldest living daughter, who was now 21, came along also. Mr. Barnum was very happy to be able to let the audiences see not only Eng and Chang but also their beautiful daughters.

On December 5, 1868, just before noon, the twins and their daughters boarded the steamer *Iowa*, in New York harbor. They were to sail at noon with their destination being Liverpool. Nannie kept a diary of the trip. She was seasick most of the two-week journey. Both Eng and Chang continuously puffing on cigars and playing chess seemed to be in the best of health.

The Bunkers were greeted in England with very cold and foggy weather. Very soon they headed to Scotland to talk with the famous doctors at the Edinburgh Medical College. Chang and Eng insisted that Katherine be examined first. The results were not good. Katherine was diagnosed with "pneumonary consumption," which was incurable. Some relief was possible but the end would be near.

Eng and Chang would be examined next. Remembering that they had been examined by hundreds, if not thousands of doctors in their lives, they were hoping that this time just might be different.

With the doctors wanting to do additional tests, Eng and Chang had to wait until after the Christmas holidays to learn of their results. In the meantime they began their exhibiting which gave them a chance to forget about the surgical possibilities. With this being Nannie's first trip to appear before an audience, she found the experience very frightening. However, the newspaper reporters were very kind in reporting the grace and charm that both Nannie and Kate presented, while at the same time praising their families back in North Carolina for having raised such fine young daughters. The remarks boosted Kate's spirits and offered Nannie confidence.

With the results from the examinations, there was little that would boost the twins' confidence. Sir James Simpson concluded that the separation could be possible, but that it would be "so perilous in its character that the twins could not, in my opinion, be justified in submitting to it, not any surgeon justified in performing it." Strangely enough, Dr. Simpson also felt it was not Eng's and Chang's desire to be separated but rather that of "some of their relatives." They twins were shocked. Even though Sarah and Adelaide had voiced that wish many times, Eng and Chang truly wanted it themselves. But he decision was clear, there would be no operation.

Being eager to get Kate home safely, the Bunkers sailed for New York on July 30, 1869. Sixteen days later they were back in Mount Airy. Nannie was happy to open her trunk containing over 100 gifts for the relatives. There were skit hoops, plaid vests, rolls of silk, rolls of calico, rings, bracelets, books, gloves, etc. Each gift pulled from the trunk was met with not only an applause and but also loud squeals.

Sometime later, a British entertainment manager contacted the twins about returning overseas, this time to France, Germany, Russia, Spain, and Italy. This time all of the Bunker children begged to go. However, Eng chose his 21-year old son James while Chang chose his 12-year old son Albert. The boys promised to bring back presents for everyone.

In February, 1870, the four Bunkers boarded the steamer *Allemagne.* Their first stop was to be in Germany where they were found themselves booked for a three week stand at the Circus Renz. The circus featured elephants, lions, and a high wire act. Eng and Chang had never in their entire lives performed in a circus before. They appeared very stiff and very stern. They were not comfortable at all with the loud music. Even though the crowds laughed at them, the twins were miserable. This would be their first and last such experience.

This experience being very painful for Eng and Chang made them more eager to find a physician who might separate them. One noted surgeon of Berlin, asked to examine them, with the help of three other doctors. Their conclusion was that there would be no operation. Such surgery "could possibly cause the opening of the abdomen and endanger their lives," the team concluded.

There was one final hope to remain. A Dr. Rudolf Virchow was considered among the best surgeons in the world. He was the first physician to describe leukemia.

Also, he was the director of Pathological Institute in Berlin. Eng and Chang requested an examination and Dr. Virchow agreed.

The examination lasted more than an hour. The twins were irritated by the procedure, in particular Chang, who pretested fiercely when the doctor pricked his side of the connecting ligament with a needle. With all of the times that Eng and Chang had been examined, none had been has uncomfortable and intense as this one. Later the doctor wrote that the Siamese twins ". . . would allow all examinations of the cord which unites them with the greatest resistance only. Obviously, it is not only sensitivity, but mistrust and fear that the cord might be injured in some way." The twins were hoping that this examination might bring good news.

Even though the doctor was convinced that the twins had organs that were totally independent of each other, he thought that the cord between them might hold important blood vessels. And, massive bleeding could occur if the cord was cut. This would be too great of a risk. Also, considering their years, there was little that was wrong with them. The harmony between them was remarkable, but this harmony had "lately been disturbed . . . by the fact that both of them are beginning to go deaf, one more rapidly than the other." Chang was becoming hard of hearing in both ears, but Eng's growing deafness was in only his left ear, the one closer to Chang. Again the recommendation was "It was not to be." Eng and Chang's last verdict was in. The doctor had represented the final dream of freedom for them. With his report, their resources and their hopes were now depleted. They would consult no more physicians abroad. They would now resign to live out their days in the same bondage they had known all of their lives.

Even though Russia was a special treat for the Bunkers, the remainder of the European tour came to a sudden and quick end. On July 19, 1870, France declared war on Germany and all Americans were advised to go home. The Bunker's did so, leaving Germany to sail back to New York.

Eng and Chang spent a great deal of their time on the return voyage playing chess. However, on the seventh day of the trip after a game ended, Eng and Chang started to rise. Eng tried to get to his feet but Chang was unable to move. He had suffered a gradual stroke and his right arm, side, and leg were paralyzed. Medical aid was summoned on the ship but the paralysis remained. Chang was confined to his berth, and Eng, who was still healthy and active, was forced to remain beside him. After this, things were never the same.

When Eng and Chang arrived in New York in August, 1870, they knew that they would never be able to travel again. The most skillful physicians were summoned for Chang who was partially paralyzed. They remained under treatment in New York for a few days but there were no indications of improvement happening so Eng and Chang left for North Carolina.

Once the twins were reunited with their wives and children in Mount Airy, Chang placed himself under the care of Dr. Joseph Hollingsworth. It seemed that none of the medications would bring about any results. So Chang, being as discouraged as he may be, took to his bed with Eng lying alongside him. In time it had been reported the Chang was able to be up even though his left hand and leg were useless.

Now with Chang being more and more depressed, he took to drinking heavily, often becoming drunk. Of course this added to the cause of quarrels which were occurring more frequently. After one particular bitter quarrel, Chang pulled a knife and shouted, "I'm going to cut your gut out!" Reacting furiously, Eng dragged his brother to Dr. Hollingsworth and begged the doctor to separate them at once. It was even reported in one medical journal that "Eng affirmed that Chang was so bad that he could live no longer with him; and Chang stated that he was satisfied to be separated, only asking that he be given an equal chance with his brother, and that the band be cut exactly in the middle."

Dr. Hollingsworth even told them that he was so anxious to know what the connecting arm contained, that the whole medical world was waiting for them to die in order to find out their secret, which he felt that the operation would prove fatal to them both, but in the interest of science he would operate immediately.

Then, laying out "knives, saws," and other surgical equipment, the physician commanded, "Very well, just get up on the table and I'll fix you, but which would you prefer, that I should sever the flesh that connects you or cut off your heads" One will produce just about the same results as the other.

This strong statement from the doctor really took Eng and Chang by surprise and brought them to a very quick decision. They calmed down, shook hands with each other, and returned to Chang's home.

At various times when the twins saw Dr. Hollingsworth, Chang would say, "We can't live long." The doctor was always fast to reassure Chang and then promise both of them that if either were to die, he would be quick to sever them so that the living twin might have every chance to survive.

It was never expected that Chang would recover but Eng's treatment of his brother was very kind during all of the long period of his sickness. This kindness was received with warmest appreciation by Chang even though there had been many reports of his being so 'ill natured'.

In spite of the difficulties imposed by Chang's afflictions, the twins were continuously busy with their families and their farms. In 1870, Chang and Adelaide had nine of their children at home with the youngest child being only two years old. This, of course, indicated that Chang had been sexually active just a year before he suffered his stroke.

Chang's farm was doing well. He had three young black laborers, as well as his oldest son Christopher who were taking care of his house and the 200 acres of farmland. The three laborers were being paid a combined salary of $350 a year along with room and board. As reported in The Two, Chang had 1 horse, 3 mules, 6 head of cattle, 8 sheep, and 30 pigs. His farm produced 50 pounds of beeswax, 200 pounds of butter, 300 pounds of honey, 2 bushels of peas and beans, 20 bushels of Irish potatoes, 80 bushels of sweet potatoes, 50 bushels of winter wheat, 50 bushels of rye, 300 bushels of oats, and 1,500 bushels of Indian corn. He sold his orchard products for $200 and his slaughtered animals for $650. The farm earned him $2,037. His totals for the year were $23,000 which was a considerable sum in 1870.

During the same year Eng and Sarah had six children at home with the youngest being 5 years old. Even though Eng did not have anywhere near the assets that his brother possessed, his situation was still very comfortable. Aunt Grace was working as a housekeeper. Eng had one black and one white laborer along with his son James Montgomery, tending to his house and 100 acres. His two laborers along with Aunt Grace received room and board and a combined salary of $100 a year. Eng's assets included 2 horses, 3 mules, 8 head of cattle, 10 sheep, and 20 pigs. During the year his farm produced 3 pounds of beeswax, 25 pounds of wool, 72 pounds of honey, 150 pounds of butter, 2 tons of hay, 25 bushels of Irish potatoes, 60 bushels of winter wheat, 75 bushels of rye, 300 bushels of oats, and 875 bushels of Indian corn. He earned $100 from his orchard products and $150 from animals slaughtered. His income from the farm for the year was $1,535. Eng's total assets were valued at $7,000 which was less than a third of his brother's worth for the same year.

Now with the twins no longer being able to help out on their farms as they used to do, they still tried to remain active. The big outdoor activity was riding in their buggy, taking pleasure rides with their children.

Although Eng and Chang no longer corresponded with friends like they once did, they continued to have a lot of affection for their one time manager James Hale and stayed in touch with him. Through all their correspondence Eng and Chang never revealed Chang's health problem to James Hale. Once, Mr. Hale even invited them to home back to New York stay at his home. The twins did not accept the invitation. They never saw James Hale again. He continued working as a proprietor of his coffee house, a steamboat agent, head of a private mail delivery service, and finally a notary public in New York until his death at the age of ninety in 1892. In fact, the twins would never visit New York again.

In 1874 a nineteen year old young man named Shepherd Monroe Dugger was visiting Mount Airy. He was the writer who privately republished a book in Burnsville, North Carolina, which among other items of interest, was about the initial conversation between Eng and Chang and Sarah and Adelaide the very first time they meet which was at the wedding of Charles Harris and Fannie Bauguess. Later, he remembered a meeting that occurred in January 1874: "The 12th day of January, Mr. Ed Banner, of Mt. Airy, whose five brothers were my neighbors at Banner Elk, NC, took me to see the twins at Chang's house. "They received me very courteously indeed." He was the last outsider to see the twins, and write about them, before the end.

The Exit to the Final Resting Place

The years were 1874 to 1917...

On Monday night, January 13, 1874, the twins were at Chang's house. Chang began coughing, "a dry cough with scanty, frothy sputum." Then he began to suffer chest pains. A family member was sent to Mount Airy to summons the family physician, Dr. Joseph Hollingsworth, to come to check on Chang. Dr. Joseph Hollingsworth was not at home, but his brother and partner, Dr. William Hollingsworth, who sometimes doctored the twins, responded at once. Upon arriving at Chang's house, Dr. Hollingsworth examined Chang and found that he was suffering from an attack of bronchitis. He also found that Eng was unaffected and was in the best of health. The doctor ordered Chang to keep warm and stay indoors until he recovered.

Dr. Joseph Hollingsworth

During the next two days, Chang remained confined and Eng was honoring Chang's every wish because they were in Chang's residence. By Wednesday, the bronchitis had subsided and Chang was feeling slightly better.

On Thursday, January, 15, Chang's condition was now stable. And as the evening was nearing, it was time for the twins to change houses as they had done without fail for many years. They were expected to spend the next three days at Eng's house. They had continued this rotation without failure for many years.

Even though Chang was ready to make the change, Adelaide objected. It was a very cold January evening, and Chang was still coughing and really was too sick to travel. Eng even tried to convince Chang not to go outdoors. Eng thought they should stay at Chang's house until Chang had fully recovered.

Chang would not agree to any part of this plan. He insisted that they stand by their agreement, three days in his house and three days in Eng's. Finally both Adelaide and Eng gave up in their attempt to convince Chang not to go outside. Eng and Chang left in their horse and carriage to go to Eng's house in order to fulfill the house rotation agreement. The houses were located over a mile apart by way of the winding road. It was very cold with wintery conditions. It took the twins about an hour to make the trip.

When they reached Eng's house, Sarah had a hot supper waiting for them. Throughout the meal, Chang complained with chills and that he was very cold. Eng and

Chang sat before a roaring fire in the parlor for a long time. Finally, late in the night, Chang agreed to go with Eng to their bed.

On Friday, January 16, after retiring for the evening, Eng fell off to sleep, but Chang was very restless. Within a short while, Chang woke Eng stating that he was having difficulty breathing. Together the twins got out of bed and made their way outside to a porch where Chang could breathe some of the cold, fresh air. They drank some water while on the porch, went back inside, and returned to their bed again. Eng dozed off immediately. Chang could not sleep. Soon after midnight, Chang woke Eng. Again they removed themselves from the bed, added logs to the fire, and sat watching the flames flicker against the wood. Finally Eng persuaded Chang to go back to bed. It was an hour or so past midnight. Eng dropped off into a deep sleep immediately.

About four in the morning, Eng's son William awakened and looked in on the two men. He found his father snoring. Yet when he turned on the kerosene lamp and went to the other side of the bed to check on his uncle, he found that Chang was not breathing. Lighting the lamp had awakened Eng.

"William, I feel a might sick," said Eng. Then he asked, "How is your Uncle Chang?"
William responded, "Uncle Chang is cold. Uncle Chang is dead."
Being alarmed, Eng looked at his brother very closely, "Then I am going!" he said.

William quickly turned and left the room. Shortly, everyone in the house was awake. Sarah sent one of the children off on a three-mile trip to Mount Airy to summon Dr. Hollingsworth. She realized that Eng was still alive. And, she remembered the doctor's brother had promised that if one of the twins died he would operate in an attempt to save the other twin from death.

Sarah immediately sat by Eng, rubbing his arms and legs as he requested. "I am very bad off," he whispered, while a cold sweat was covering his body. His children took turns rubbing his body. The minutes were ticking away.

Eng gazed at his brother. Sixty-three years they had been together. Now he pulled his brother to him in a final embrace. Looking around at his family, Eng whispered, "May the Lord have mercy on my soul." Those were his last words.

He lapsed into a coma like "stupor." It had been an hour since Chang's death had been discovered. Eng continued to lie in a stupor for another hour. Then he died. Just as Eng had lived his life with his brother Chang, he had died with him, too. It was January 17, 1874.

Adelaide was summoned and expressed strong disappointment that she had not been sent for earlier. The doctor arrived carrying his surgical instruments, but there was no need for the surgical instruments.

Later that day the wives prepared their husbands for public viewing. Friends and neighbors would want to pay their respects.

Dr. Hollingsworth and others expressed concerns as to whether or not that there should be any type of postmortem to determine the cause of death for both men. The widows wanted no part of this. Then, the idea arose concerning the possibility of vandalism. Would the bodies of Eng and Chang ever be safe from grave robbers? Would the corpses be stolen and exhibited? Since the burial site could not be protected forever, this terrible act of theft was bound to occur sooner or later. The Dr. Hollingsworth even offered a sensible suggestion to Sarah and Adelaide. And that was for them to legitimately sell their husbands' corpses for exhibition. This was a suggestion to not only generate money for the families, but also to gain some "sense of security" that the bodies could not fall into the hands of thieves.

The wives finally decided that the oldest son of each family help make the decision for final disposition. The doctor agreed, but reminded the widows that the bodies needed to be preserved and would also need to be buried in a temporary place that could be protected. With no means to embalm the bodies, it was decided that the bodies could be sealed in a walnut casket, which in turn would be placed inside a tin coffin, and then placed in a wooden box. This triple coffin would be buried in the basement of Eng's home. It was cool there, and the bodies would be preserved until it was safe to bury the twins in a permanent spot elsewhere.

As soon as these decisions were made, a William Augustus Reich was asked to make a tin coffin large enough to hold the twins' casket. William stated in a letter to his sister that he had to cut 34 big sheets of tin to make the coffin. Also, he asked her if she thought that $20 would be too much to charge. Later in the letter, William concluded that this was the greatest job that he had ever done and, "It was a sight to see the people that came to my house to see me make the coffin."

On Sunday, January 18, rumors were spreading over Surry County that the funeral would be held on that day and that the public would be able to view the bodies. A very large crowd gathered outside Eng's home, including clergyman. Finally the door to the house was opened and the crowd poured inside. After viewing the bodies, the crowd was informed that the funeral had been postponed until a later date. With this information, the crowd soon left.

Sarah and Adelaide soon would be facing another decision. A Dr. William Pancoast of Philadelphia, representing many other noted physicians, asked if they might be granted permission to examine the bodies of Eng and Chang. Finally secrets of the connecting ligaments would be explored, secrets that had held mysteries of physicians for approximately 50 years.

The widows agreed. First, Dr. Pancoast arrived to examine the bodies in Mount Airy. It was quickly determined that Eng's home was not suitable for a complete examination. The bodies were embalmed and shipped to the Mutter Museum of the College of Physicians in Philadelphia.

The findings were announced on February 18, 1874. The doctors discovered that the livers of both men "pushed through the respective peritoneal openings into the band." In other words, the flesh that joined Eng and Chang contained very important liver tissue. The twins could have died in any operation. The final conclusion from the doctors was that Chang had died of a cerebral blood clot, while Eng died of shock and fright.

The autopsy did make three points concerning the separation question. Separation as children might have been wise; no such operation could have been worth the risk later in life; and the operation should have been performed immediately upon Chang's death. In 1897, the American Medical Association weighed in for a final judgment: Given advances in the use of antiseptics, had the twins lived at that time, they could have been successfully separated.

The doctors at the Mutter Museum asked to keep the joined livers of the twins. The organs could be preserved in formalin. But when the bodies of Eng and Chang were returned to Mount Airy, it was discovered that the lungs and intestines were missing. Once more the Siamese twins posed another mystery, even after their deaths. Members of the Bunker family demanded explanations, but it was never determined what had happened to these body parts.

After the autopsy of Eng and Chang, the bodies were returned and buried back in the dirt cellar of Eng's house.

When the bodies were returned to Mount Airy, it was not considered safe to bury them immediately still considering the danger of grave robbers. A local newspaper reported that for a year the bodies were kept in the cellar of Eng's house, the casket covered with charcoal and heavily guarded by the family day and night. After about a year, they were buried on the lawn near Chang's house.

Interestingly enough, the bodies of Eng and Chang remained in the grave on Chang's lawn until Chang's wife, Adelaide died on May 21, 1917.

Gravestone of Eng and Chang Bunker placed at their grave which is in the front yard of Chang's house. Notice the picket fence in the background that is so visible in the older pictures of Chang's home.

This was almost forty three years after their death. When the time came to bury Adelaide, one of her sons-in-law, Caleb Hill Haynes, who was married to one of her daughters, Margaret Elizabeth, suggested that since White Plains Baptist Church had meant so much to Adelaide for most of her lifetime, it seemed to be appropriate to bury her in the cemetery of that church. And, he also suggested, that since Chang's farm, where the twins were buried, could one day become, the property of someone else, it might be well to move the bodies of Eng and Chang to the church graveyard along with Adelaide. Also, the twins had donated the land to the church when it was built and also included enough for a large graveyard. The family members agreed to this.

So, according to Irving Wallace in his book, The Two, ". . . on May 17, 1917, the walnut coffin containing the bodies of Eng and Chang was unearthed and lifted out of the plot beside the holly tree on the front lawn of Chang's house. Apparently the bodies of the twins were briefly exposed to sight, for one witness recalled that "when they were dug up to be reburied there were very few bones, a little hair, and a shoe heel with nails in it." Then the coffin was closed.

It has been reported that there were two sets of horse and wagon teams available for moving the two coffins containing three bodies to the cemetery. As the coffin of Eng and Chang was being moved from Chang's property to the White Plains Baptist Church cemetery, a white dove flew down, lighted on the coffin and rested there throughout the one mile trip to the church. While the coffin was being unloaded and moved to the grave, the dove still remained on the coffin. And, it sat there until the coffin began to be lowered in the grave. Then it flew away. Adelaide, Eng and Chang were all buried at White Plains on the same day in May of 1917.

Now if one visits the cemetery at White Plains and looks at the monument of the twins, one must know that Eng's wife, Sarah, has never been buried at White Plains Church Cemetery even though her information is on the monument. Sarah died at the age of seventy. For some unknown reason, her body is buried on Eng's farm with her own gravestone there. Much speculation suggest that Sarah had two babies buried close by that area when the foursome first moved to White Plains and that she wanted to be buried close to her babies. Another story suggest that some slaves are buried in that same area and that since the slaves had been so good to the Bunker Family that Sarah wanted to be buried close to them. So, as the reader, you will need to form your own conclusion.

There are thousands of sightseers who visit the White Plains Baptist Church Cemetery each year. And, many wonder aloud, "How many brothers could claim the same birth date and death date"?

White Plains Baptist Church Cemetery is a peaceful resting place for the "Chinese boys from Siam" who were just two men living as one. The lived and died as they had always done everything else , together. Today, the state of North Carolina has a historical marker (pictured above) posted outside the White Plains Baptist Church.

> **"We came into this world together, and lived it together, and so it shall be that we leave it together".**

It is believed that as of the completion of this book in 2013, that Eng and Chang Bunker are holding at least three world records from their miraculous births and lives.

1. They are the only conjoined twins to live as long as they did—63 years.

2. They are the only conjoined twins to marry.

3. They are the only conjoined twins to father children.

Also, it is believed that as of this writing, there are over 1500 documented descendants of Eng and Sarah and Chang and Adelaide Bunker. The last Thursday, Friday, and Saturday of July each summer, several hundred of these descendants gather in Mount Airy, NC, for the annual reunion of "The Descendants of Eng and Chang Bunker."

In North Carolina, they sleep their eternal sleep together. In the world, they live, perhaps, forever.

From the book - THE TWO

The Bunker Family Album

The Personal
Photo & Document
Collection
of
Author Melvin M. Miles

The World Famous Eng and Chang Bunker

First Home In Traphill, North Carolina

Inside the home in Traphill, Wilkes County, North Carolina

Stairs 42" wide   *Railing Post at top of stairs*

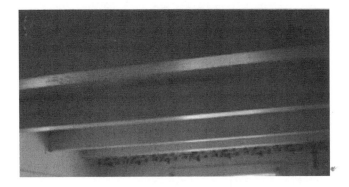

Ceiling Beams from the original home of Eng and Chang

Pictured above are two hand hewed stones that were very near a stream at Eng and Chang's home in Traphill. The long and more narrow container is about 5 feet long and maybe 24 inches wide. There are grooves at each end of the box for water to enter and drain. This would be used to keep items cool such as milk in containers. The other box was deep enough for one to gather a bucket of water with one dip. This was to be carried into the house for inside use - before indoor plumbing. These containers have been moved closer to the house into a side yard today. They will be incorporated into a nearby stream as the house is being turned into a "bed and breakfast".

Eng & Chang   *Sarah & Adelaide*

Eng (left) with wife Sarah and son Patrick;
Chang (right) with wife Adelaide and son Albert

First Home of Eng and Sarah Bunker
White Plains, North Carolina. Built about 1847

Corn crib of Eng   *Home destroyed by fired 1957*

Home of Chang and Adelaide. Built about 1857 White Plains, North Carolina. It was the Second home built when the twins divided the farm.

Home of Chang and Adelaide, as it is today.

Kate and Nannie

Jessie Bunker Bryant
Author of "The Connected Bunkers"

Tom Bunker, Hubert Bunker, Ed Bunker, Nan Bunker Atkins,
John Bunker, Kate Bunker Cross, Albert Bunker, and Sally
Bunker Cockerham

(Left) Susan Bunker, wife of Steven Bunker
(Right) Fannie Bunker, wife of Robert Bunker

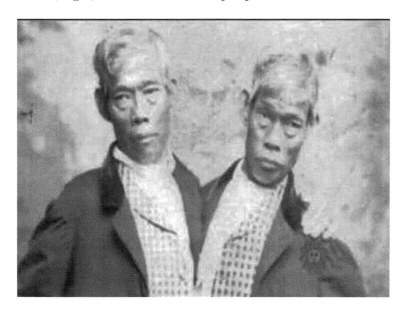

Eng & Chang

*Ralph Bunker, sixth child of Robert Edward and Fannie Bunker,
at work as Master Carver in Jacksonville, FL, 1960.*

Adelaide Bunker at the front door of her home.

Lucy (family friend), Carrie Haynes (granddaughter of Chang), and Lucy's Mother

Robert Edward Bunker
Youngest child of Eng and Sarah Bunker, working the fields.

Stephen Bunker
Son of Chang and Adelaide Bunker
Fought in the Civil War

Miss Katherine "Kate" Marcellus Bunker,
first child born to Eng and Sarah Yates Bunker in
Traphill, Wilkes County, NC

Nancy Adelaide Bunker "Nannie"
Daughter of Chang and Adelaide Bunker

Patrick Henry Bunker, Eng and Chang Bunker,
Christopher Wrenn Bunker, and Albert Bunker

Adelaide Yates Bunker
October 11, 1823 to May 21, 1917

Grace Gates,
was a slave given to Eng and Sarah as a wedding present
in 1843. She was known as "Aunt Grace". She cared
for all of the Bunker children. She died in 1921 at the
age of 121

One of the 'double chairs' of Eng and Chang

Major General Caleb V. Haynes

*United States Air Force Major General Caleb V. Haynes
was a grandson of Chang Bunker through his daughter
Margaret Elizabeth "Lizzie" Bunker.*

Alex Sink,
Great Grand-daughter of Chang and Adelaide Yates Bunker, was
married to Bill McBride, below. She was a former gubernatorial
candidate for the state of Florida. Also, Chief Financial Officer for
the state of Florida and treasurer on the Board of Trustees of the
Florida State Board of Administration.

Bill McBride, (1945-2012) was the husband of Alex Sink. He was
a prominent attorney in the state of Florida. He was also a former
gubernatorial candidate for the state of Florida.

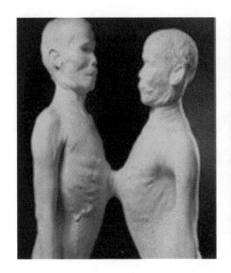
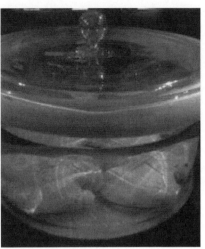

Plaster models of Eng and Chang,
along with their livers at the Mutter Museum Philadelphia,
Pennsylvania

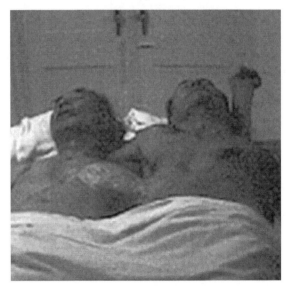

Eng and Chang
1811-1874
Together Forever

Statue of Eng & Chang
Bangkok, Thailand

Victoria, fifth child of Chang and Adelaide

Albert, Eng and Chang, unknown daughter

Louisa Bunker and husband, Zacharias Haynes
Daughter of Chang and Adelaide

Judy Ross Bunker and husband, William Oliver Bunker

Louisa Bunker and Zacharias Haynes Family

*Robert "Big Bob" Bunker, youngest son of Eng and Sarah
sitting next to the bed he was born on and died on.*

Bedroom in Eng's house

Woo Eng Bunker, Otto Jerden Bunker, Stephen Dana Bunker

Napoleon Bunker, son of William Oliver Bunker

Chris Bunker Mill

Corn Crib of Eng Bunker

Pictured are a few of the Grandchildren of Robert E. Bunker & Great Grandchildren of Eng and Sarah Yates Bunker

Left to Right Lula Bunker White, Gerald White, Hershel Bunker & wife Ethalene Bunker, Eng Bunker, and wife Francis Bunker (Combined Photo)

Left to Right: Tanya Blackmon Jones, Monty Blackmon, Betty Bunker Blackmon, Zack Blackmon, Jr., Deidre Blackmon Rogers

Robert Edward, the youngest son of Eng and Sarah Bunker, Ethel Wilson, granddaughter of Patrick Henry Bunker, and Albert Lemuel Bunker, son of Chang and Adelaide Bunker

Fannie Elizabeth Jenkins, wife of Robert Edward Bunker, youngest child of Eng and Sarah Bunker

Woo Eng Bunker, 1901-1980, was a grandson of Eng and Sarah Bunker. He was the son of Stephen Bunker and Sarah Alice Nichols Bunker, and a World War II Veteran.

Josephine Virginia Bunker
First Child of Chang and Adelaide Bunker

Betty Bunker Blackmon pictured at the grave of her Great-grandmother, Sarah Yates Bunker located in the slave cemetery

Etchings on monument of Sarah A. Bunker,
wife of Eng Bunker

Robert Bunker with his wife Fannie,
youngest son of Eng

Illustrated photograph
Eng & Chang Bunker Family

Vance Haynes is a son of United States Air Force Major General Caleb Vance Haynes. He is a great grandson of Chang Bunker through his daughter Margaret Elizabeth "Lizzie" Bunker. Mr. Haynes earned a doctorate in geosciences, performed foundational fieldwork at Sandia Cave to determine the time of human migration through North America, and served as professor at several universities including anthropology professor at the University of Arizona, Tucson, AZ.

Road sign for bridge over Stewart's Creek on Highway 601 South of Mount Airy. This is the creek which divided the two farms for Eng and Chang Bunker

Connected, Maybe - Conjoined, Definitely

Eng's home place 1941 or 1942
Left to right back row: Lurene Nichols Bunker, Edward M.
Bunker, Ethel Wilson, Woo Bunker, Robert E. Bunker son of Eng,
Winfred Cockerham, Sally Bunker Cockerham, Albert M. Bunker
son of Robert, Emma G. Bunker, Kate Bunker Cross, Lucian
Cross, Albert Bunker son of Chang. Children front row: Bobby
Bunker, Dorothy Cross, Betty Bunker, Martha Cross, Elaine
Bunker.

Descendants Luncheon Reunion 2012

Eng and Chang Bunker
first set of twins born in the line of descendants.

Albert Bunker, James Montgomery Bunker,
Eng & Chang Bunker

Silverware belonging to the Bunker's

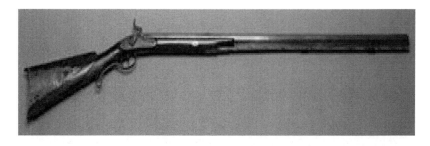

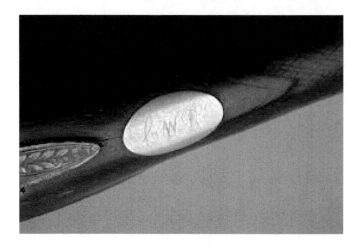

In April 2012, Chang Bunker's Rifle was donated to UNC Wilson Special Collections Libraries by Dr. Vance Haynes, a professor of archeology at the University of Arizona and Great Grandson of Chang. The rifle is in excellent condition and will likely shed new light on the lives of these legendary figures.

Fannie Bunker, wife of Robert Bunker, holding her great-granddaughter Betty Bunker Blackmon

*White Plains Baptist Church and cemetery located on Old HWY
601 Mount Airy, NC. Siamese Twins burial place.
Eng & Chang donated land for the cemetery.*

The Siamese Twins with their Wives and 18 of their 21 Children

Not pictured (Katherine, 1844-1871), (Rosalyn 1852-1852), (Georginia 1863-1865)

Eng

Victoria

Julia Ann

Susan Mariana

Chang

Patrick Henry

Adelaide

Louisa Emaline

Margaret Elizabeth

Aunt Grace

Hattie Irene

Steven Decatur

Sarah

Frederick Marshall

Robert Edward

Rosella Virginia

Jesse Lafayette

Nancy Adelaide

Albert Lemuel

Christopher Wrenn

Josephine Virginia

James Montgomery

William Oliver

We the undersigned Chang & Eng agree, bind & engage ourselves, with our own free will & consent (also that we have the free will & consent of our Parents and the King of our country), to go with Capt. Abel Coffin to America and Europe and remain with them wherever he chooses, until the expiration of the time agreed upon between Capt. Coffin and the Gov of our country; and that he according to promise will return us to our Parents & friends in time within five (5) Years, and that Capt. Coffin will allow us, from his Profits ten Spanish $ Month, and pay all our expenses, and nothing is to be deducted for the money allowed our mother dated in Bangkock, first day of April one Thousand Eight Hundred & twenty nine

Chang's signature Eng's signature

見曾因洽吾我天成

[witness]

At the request of Capt. Coffin I have translated the above to the Boys, & they are fully satisfied with the contents, Bangkock 1st April 1829

Rob Hunter

Wm. Markt. Bangkok

Contract of Eng and Chang to exhibit with
Robert Hunter, the sea merchant.

Madison Village, Madison Co.
27th July 1832.   N.Y.

Dear Sir,

I fully expected to have heard from you during our stay in Utica, but have been unfortunately disappointed; Chang-Eng fully expect, from this, that Captn. Coffin is come home & have asked me to write to you again to let you know our intended movements.

Our movements at present are through County Villages, for in all large Towns the panic is so great that people are not much inclined for amusement; but I am happy to say that in the Villages Chang-Eng do remarkably well — as their receipts are considerable & their expenses light. However I shall give you a sketch of our intended movements for some time to come—

On Wed. & Th. 1st & 2nd August — we shall be at "Log City"
On Fri. & Sat. 3rd & 4th " ———— " ———— Morrisville
On Mon. & Tu. 6th & 7th " ———— " ————
On Wed. & Th. 8th & 9th " ———— " ———— Cazenovia
On Fri. & Sat. 10th & 11th " ———— " ———— Woodstock
                                                    De Ruyter
N.B. all the above are in Madison County — N.Y.

If on receipt of this you should wish to write, you can direct to me at Woodstock or De Ruyter in Madison County — N.Y. at which places I shall leave our address so that any letter may be forwarded in case they should reach either of those Villages after our Departure;
If at any time you should be hereafter at a loss to know our intended movements, I would recommend you to forward your letter to Mr. Hale at Boston who generally knows from Chang-Eng our movement — as they often communicate with him generally once a week. —
I have taken care that all letters sent to Utica shall be forwarded to us. — I am sorry I did not hear from you during our stay in Utica — as I could have made a remittance from that place of the remainder of the Balance of money belonging to the Concern of Mr. C — had so wished it ———

Letter from Charles Harris to Captain Coffin

State of North Carolina Fall Term 1839
Wilkes County } Superior Court of Law

Chang—Eng (commonly known as the Siamese twins) represent to this Honourable Court, that they are natives of the kingdom of Siam in Asia—that they arrived in Boston, in the state of Massachusetts (U.S.) on the 16th of August 1829 In October of that year they went to England and returned to the United States in March 1831. & resided therein without leaving them until the Fall of 1835 when they went to Lower Canada Soon after went to the Continent of Europe and were absent about 12 months.— After their return in 1836 they went to the Province of Lower Canada when they remained until October 1836 when they returned to the United States & have continued therein without leaving them ever since & since the 1st day of June 1839 have continued within the State of North Carolina They further represent that during their continuance within the United States they have behaved as men of good moral characters, that they are attached to the principles of the constitution of the United States and are well disposed to the good order and happiness of the same.—And they here before this Honl court declare their intention to become citizens of the United States, and to renounce his allegiance to the King of Siam & any other state, king, sovereignty—And respectfully pray that this Honorable court may receive this their declaration made before this court with the view of becoming naturalized citizens of the United States & that the same be made a record thereof be made—such such order & judgment in the premises as is by law required —

Chang Eng

Sworn to before me

Eng and Chang's Application for Citizenship

186

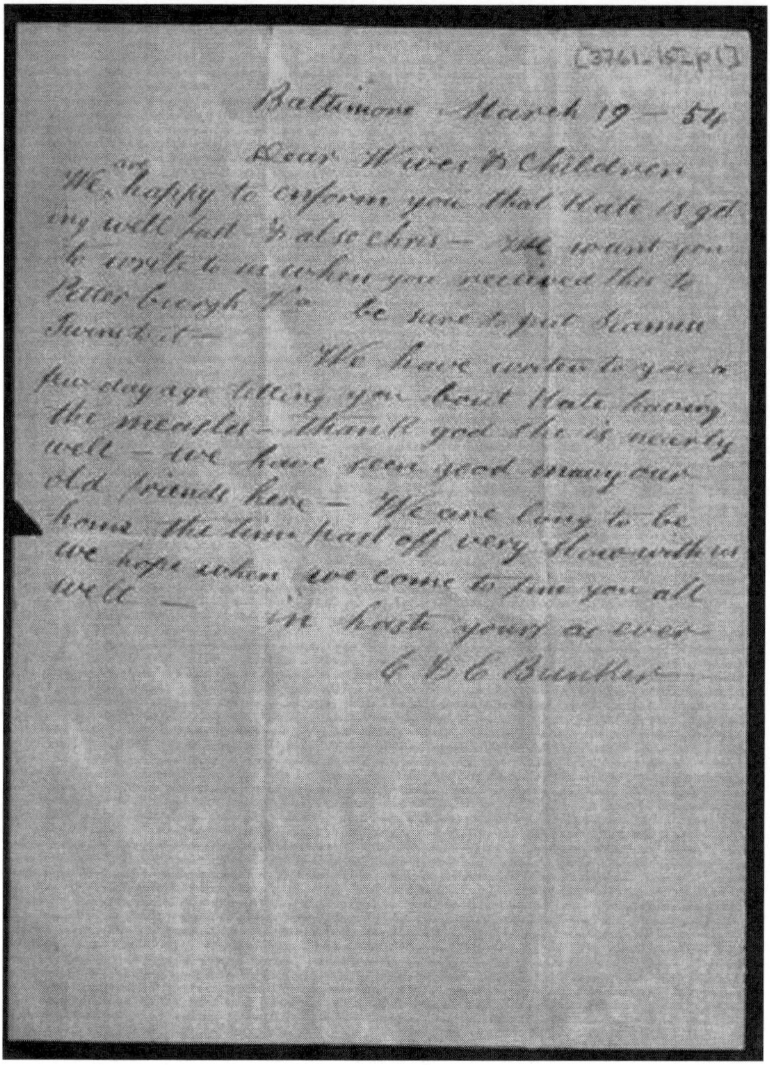

[3761-152 p(1)]

Baltimore March 19 — 54

Dear Wives & Children

We are happy to inform you that Kate is get-
ing well fast & also Chris — We want you
to write to us when you received this to
Petersburgh Va be sure to put Gammu
Turnit it —

We have written to you a
few days ago telling you bout Kate having
the measles — thank god she is nearly
well — we have seen good many our
old friends here — We are long to be
home the time past off very slow with us
we hope when we come to find you all
well —

in haste yours as ever

C & E Bunker —

Letter from Eng and Chang
to their wives and children.

Chang Bunker from Eng Bunker bill of sale 10 Slaves

Whereas a copartnership has heretofore existed between Eng & Chang Bunker in the following negro slaves to wit 1 Berry a man aged about 60 years

2 Jean a girl " " 30 years

3 Daniel Boy " " 17 years

4 Nice " gal " " 16 years

5 Shuman " Boy " " 12 years

6 Moses " Boy " " 12 years

7 Patie " Girl " " 11 years

8 Perry " Boy " " 9 years

9 Alen or Creey a gal " " 8 years

10 Carline " gal " 6 years

And whereas it is mutually agreed by and between the parties that the said Chang Bunker is to have the full and entire interest in said Negro Slaves This indenture therefore witnesseth that the said Eng Bunker for and in consideration of the sum of one Dollar to him in hand paid by the said Chang Bunker the receipt whereof is hereby fully acknowledged hath sold and delivered to the said Chang Bunker and his heirs and assigns forever the undivided one half of the aforesaid slaves

In testimony whereof the said Eng Bunker hath hereto set his hand and seal this 20th November AD 1855 Eng Bunker (seal)

Test Job Worth pres

William Nawley

North Carolina Mecy Term 1859 the Execution of the foregoing bill

Bill of Sale for slave trade

188

Camp Chase O., Oct the 12th 1864

Dear Father, Mother, Brothers and Sisters

It is with pleasure I take the present opportunity to drop you a few lines to let you know how I am getting along. I was captured the 7th of last August and brought to this place. I have no news of interest to write to you as there are none allowed to come in prison. You must write to me as soon as you get this and let me know how you are getting along. I would like to hear from you all as it has been a long time since I heard from you and I hope it will not be very long before I hear from you and see you too, all though I see no chance for no an exchange.

I have not seen many well days since I came to this place. I have had the Small pox and have now got the diarea but I hope that I will be well in the course of a week. The Smallpox did not go very hard with me it did not confine me to my bed but about three weeks. I would like to have some cloths as I have not got but one suit and and it is very thin summer goods but it is impossible for you to send me any from home. We are drawing very light rations here just enough to keep breath and body together. I must bring this to a close and I hope it will find you well and doing well. Direct to Camp Chase Columbus Ohio and put it in another envelop and direct to Judge Ould Officer of exchang Richmond Va

I remain your son ever C W Bunker

Letter from Chris Bunker to family while being a Prisoner of War during the Civil War

North Carolina State Board of Health
BUREAU OF VITAL STATISTICS
CERTIFICATE OF DEATH

123

PLACE OF DEATH
County Surry
Township Mt Airy
Town Mt Airy
Registration District No. 86-9063
Certificate No. 37
City
R. F. D. 4

FULL NAME Adelaide Bunker

PERSONAL AND STATISTICAL PARTICULARS

SEX female
COLOR OR RACE White
SINGLE, MARRIED, WIDOWED, or DIVORCED Widower

DATE OF BIRTH October 11, 823

AGE 93 yrs 7 mos 10 days

OCCUPATION House Keeper

EDUCATIONAL ATTAINMENTS Common school

BIRTHPLACE Wilkes Co N.C.

NAME OF FATHER David Yates
BIRTHPLACE OF FATHER N.C.
MAIDEN NAME OF MOTHER Hayes
BIRTHPLACE OF MOTHER N.C.

THE ABOVE IS TRUE TO THE BEST OF MY KNOWLEDGE
(Informant) C. H. Haynes
(Address) Mt Airy N.C.
Filed May 22, 17 E. A. Hannah Registrar

MEDICAL CERTIFICATE OF DEATH

DATE OF DEATH May 21, 17

I HEREBY CERTIFY, That I attended deceased from March 2nd, 17 to May 21st, 17
that I last saw h.r. alive on May 20
and that death occurred on the date above, at 7:45 a.m.
The CAUSE OF DEATH was as follows:
General debility
no disease

(Signed) W. S. Taylor, M.D.
May 22, 17 Mt Airy

PLACE OF BURIAL OR REMOVAL White Plains
DATE OF BURIAL May 22nd, 17
UNDERTAKER E. A. Hannah
ADDRESS Mt Airy N.C.

Death Certificate of Adelaide Yates Bunker
wife of Chang Bunker
Age 93 years, 7 months, 10 days

Transcription of Eng Bunker's Will

I Eng Bunker of the County of Surry and state of North Carolina being of sound mind and memory and knowing the uncertainty of all human e vents and especially life do make and declare this to be my last will and testament constitute and appoint my beloved wife Sally Ann Bunker my true and lawful executrix who after paying the necessary expenses of a decent burial for myself shall pay all my just and lawful debts out of my personal estate.

Item I bequeath and devise to my wife Sally Ann Bunker on account of the tender love and affection I have for her All my lands to have and to hold and enjoy during her natural life and should my beloved wife Sally Ann Bunker die before my minor children because of age then it is my desire that the lands remain unsold in order that my minor children may enjoy the rent and profits of my land and may have a home during their infancy and after the death of my wife and after my infant children shall become of age then the said land may be equally divided among all my children.

Item I will bequeath and devise all my house hold and kitchen furniture all horses cows pigs and all cattle of whatsoever kind that is now on the farm also all farming utensils to my wife during her life and after her death should she die before my infant children come of age it is my desire that the above named personal property remains for the benefit of my infant children and that none of the above mentioned property be sold until after the death of my wife and until the minor children shall become of age.

Item --I will and bequeath all my money that may be on hand or owed the estate at my death to be divided among my children equally and it is further my desire that after the death of my wife and after my minor children shall become of age that all my property both real and personal be equally divided among all my children. In testimony whereof I have put into act my hand and seal this 27th day of November A.D. 1868

We the undersigned (seal) do affix our names as (signed) Eng Bunker Witnesses in the presence and at the request of the testator to his last will and testament.

Robert S Gilmer   (signed) H. O. Allred

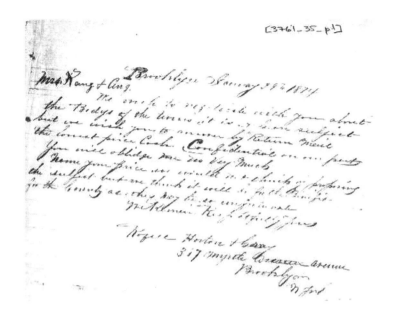

Letter to Sarah and Adelaide from people in New York City
requesting a price for the deceased bodies of Eng and Chang.
(Transcribed below)

January 29ᵀᴴ 1874

Mrs. Kang and Ang
We wish to negotiate with you about the body's of the twins it is a
(?) subject but we wish you to answer by Return Mail the lowest
price Cash. Confidential on our part you will oblige us very much.
Name your price. We would not think of proposing the subject but
we think it will be for the Benefit for the County as others may be
so unfortunate.

We Remain Respectfully Yours
Rozell, Horton and Gray

387 Myrtle Avenue
Brooklyn N York

Transcription of Chang Bunker's Will

I Chang Bunker of Surry and State of North Carolina being of sound mind and memory and knowing the uncertainty of my earthly existence do make and declare this to be my last will and testament in manner and form as follows that is to say.

First –I will and devise to my wife Adelaide Bunker on account of the love and affection I have for her, all my lands to have hold and enjoy during her natural life and should my wife Adelaide Bunker die before my minor children because of age then it is my will and desire that my lands remain unsold and the rents and profits thereof be expended for the maintenance, support and education of all my children who shall remain single and unmarried and should the rents and profits of my lands be more than necessary for the support of my single and infant children and wife then it is my will and desire that the remainder of the rents be equally divided among all my children and after the death of my wife and after all my infant children shall have arrived at full age then I will and devise all my lands to all my children equally to have and to hold to them and their heirs in full transfer forever.

Item – I will and bequeath that after my death all my personal property of whatever kind and description shall be divided equally among all my children and wife except – my two dumb children Louisa E. Bunker and Jessie L. Bunker who shall have five hundred each more than any of the rest of my children on account of their affliction to have and to hold to them and their heirs and Assigns absolutely and forever and it is my desire and wish that in the distribution and division of my personal property that each one of my children account for the property – they have secured at the valuation I have set upon it which prices on records in a book kept for that purpose.

In testimony I have herewith set my hand and seal this 15th day of May 1871 – Chang Bunker (seal)

Witnesses :

Joseph Hollingsworth

R. S. Gilmer

The story of the journey from Siam to Surry . . .

. . . is continuing to travel to all parts of the world.

APPENDIX A

The Yates' side of the Family

David Yates was born in 1795 in Wilkes County, North Carolina, and died in 1851 in Wilkes County. His father was John Yates, Jr. who was born in 1780, Caswell County, NC. His mother was Elizabeth Cleveland, who was born in 1783 in Wilkes County, NC. He married Nancy Hayes Yates on October 22, 1814 in Wilkes County. She was born in 1794 and died in 1850.

David Yates was not only a farmer and a church-going Baptist preacher, but also a county justice. He was of Dutch and Irish descent. He and his wife had six children. They are:

--Alston Yates (1816-January 15, 1898) married Elizabeth Holbrook (1838-1918) daughter of Caleb Holbrook and Mary Winfrey

--Jesse Yates (March 4, 1817-1862) married Sarah Caroline Eller (June 14, 1831-May 27, 1919). They were parents of 13 children.

--Letha Yates (1821 - January 24, 1910) married Samuel J. Bauguess (about 1817) A brother to Fannie Bauguess, who married Charles Harris, the manager of Eng and Chang Bunker for many years.

--Sarah Ann Yates (December 18, 1822- April 29, 1892) married Eng Bunker.

-- Adelaide Yates (October 11, 1823- May 21, 1917) married Chang Bunker.

--Jerusha Yates (1828-abt. 1900) married Robert Yates, her first cousin. He was the son of John Yates and Elizabeth Cleveland.

The future of the Yates' family and Eng and Chang began when their great friend and previous manager Charles Harris married Fannie Bauguess. This wedding took place in the Traphill community at the home of Robert Bauguess where Charles Harris, along with Eng and Chang Bunker, had rented rooms. This was also very close to where Eng and Chang had purchased land from Robert Bauguess and built their first home.

After a lot of dialogue, visiting, meeting in secret, and convincing the Yates' parents, the girls finally consented to get married. Sarah married Eng and Adelaide married Chang.

After the twins realized that the Yates sisters lived between Traphill and Wilkesboro, it was rather easy for the twins to stop by for visits on their way to and from town. At a later time, as the twins were passing the Yates farm, they were invited to come into the house to meet Adelaide and Sarah's mother, Nancy, with whom Eng and Chang found they had something in common. Mrs. Yates was also a local curiosity—she was about five feet seven inches in height and nearly nine feet in circumference. Her accurate weight was never measured because there were no adequate means of weighing her in that neighborhood. It was believed that she was very possibly the largest woman in the state of North Carolina, possibly in America. She weighed over 500 pounds and never left home. She died of obesity. The door of the house had to be altered in order to remove her body for burial.

David and his wife were very successful farmers who had a large white house and slave cabins for 15 slaves on a hillside overlooking their 1200+ acres of farmland located six miles outside of Wilkesboro in the Mulberry Creek community. David Yates enjoyed Eng and Chang visiting when traveling to and from Wilkesboro so he could give them advice about their ever-growing farm in Traphill. Their farm started with 150 acres. The brothers bought any adjoining property that became available for sale. They bought one plot which had 26 ½ acres and soon another measuring 37 ½ acres. The twins did raise corn and hogs at the time.

While there was some objection over the marriage due to both ethnicity and the twins being conjoined, the girl's parents consented eventually. The wedding of Eng and Sarah and Chang and Adelaide took place on April 13, 1843, in the living room of the Yates farmhouse.

Eng and Sarah became parents to 11 children, 6 boys and 5 girls. Chang and Adelaide became parents to 10 children, 3 boys and 7 girls. As the children were born, name selection became a challenge for both families. Family and friends received first consideration, while Sarah and Adelaide often wanted Biblical names since they were from a strict Baptist background and had attended church whenever they could. Eng and Chang preferred names of either famous people, or people who had been heroes in history.

The following pages contain part of a family tree of the Yates' families. This writer does not guarantee that all of this information is correct, but it is the information that could be located.

John Yates Family of Wilkes County, NC

John Yates, Sr. married Jemima Roper on March 8, 1779, in Caswell County, North Carolina. They settled on the north fork of Lewis Creek in Wilkes County about 1835 and Jemima died after 1851.

1. Children of John Yates, Sr. (Mar, 1754, Halifax, VA - Died December 16, 1835, Wilkes County, NC) m. Jemima Roper (1755, Orange, NC - May 02, 1853, Wilkes County, NC). She was the daughter of David Roper and Sarah Yates.

NOTE: John Yates, Sr., was a Revolutionary War Migration who moved to Wilkes Co., NC, before 1776 prior to that he was in Caswell Co. BC. He returned to Caswell Co. to marry Jemima Roper and brought her back to Wilkes Co. Place North Fork of Lewis Fork Creek had 400 acres of land. Birthplace is part of what is now Pittsylvania Co., VA June 1, 1767.

John Yates, Jr. (1780, Lewis Fork, Wilkes, NC -Died February 06, 1875, Wilkes, NC) m. 'Elizabeth Cleveland D 82-1850); 2) Fannie Lamira Laws (1823-1912), d/o Levi Laws and Margaret Church.

> Children of John Yates, Jr. and his 1st wife Elizabeth Cleveland
> 2-1 Sarah Yates (1804-1877) m George McGlamery (abt. 1795-1850)
> 2-2 Presley Yates (1806-1878) m. Rachel Thedford
> 2-3 David Yates (1808-1860) m. Elizabeth Church (abt. 1817-aft. 1850), d/o John Church and Sarah Billings
> 3-1 Laura Yates (abt. 1849-aft. 1850).
> 2-4 Barnard Yates (1810-1854) m. 1) Mary Vannoy; 2) Nancy Eller
> 2-5 Frances Yates (1815-bf. 1850) m. Peter Eller
> 2-6 Jesse Yates (1817-1891) m. Sarah Caroline Eller (1831-

1919), d/o John Eller and Sarah Vannoy. Jesse was a school teacher and a farmer in Wilkes County

3-1 Elizabeth Yates

3-2 Finley Gordon Yates (abt. 1852-1936) not married in 1920).

3-3 Lelia Jane Yates (abt. 1852-aft. 1860) m Berryman Fletcher (abt. 1837-aft 1880), s/o of Joshua Fletcher and Margaret Laws Church

3-4 Leander Carmichael Yates (abt. 1854-aft. 1920) m. Jestine Martha Phills (abt. 1876-aft. 1920)

3-5 Jesse Vannoy Yates (abt. 1857-1926) m. Sarah Jane Miller (1860-1938).

    4-1 Mordecal Nehemiah Yates m. Georgia Howard

    4-2 Alice Yates m. Charles Greever Hartson

    4-3 Benjamin Cleveland Yates (1884-1977) m. Mary Lora Rettie Rash (1892- ?) d/o Alexander and Lila Richardson Rash)

        5-1 Clara Alice Rash m. Charles Hensley

        5-2 Eunice Bessie Rash m. Glenn Thomas Barker

        5-3 James Vasco Rash m. Ruth Kille

        5-4 Della Grace Rash m Wade H. Jones, Jr.

        5-5 Sarah Irene Rash m. Russell Jones

        5-6 Florence Esther Rash m. Fred Ashley

        5-7 Ella Hattie Rash died young

        5-8 Elmer Reece Rash m. Hazel Childers

        5-9 Lora Jane Rash died young

    4-4 Mack Vanderbilt (Van) Yates

    4-5 Bina Yates died in childhood

    4-6 Davie Yates died in childhood

    4-7 John Edward Yates died of pneumonia while serving with the Armed Forces during WWI

        4-8 George F. Yates.

        4-9 Roy E. Yates.

        4-10 James Finley Yates (Jim) also served in the

Armed Forces during WWI. He then owned and
operated a store in Warrensville for many
years.

        4-11 Dewey Harrison Yates (Shorty).

        4-12 Ora Esther Yates m. Tyre Lee Rash

        4-13 Hattie Margaret Yates m. Cicero Johnson

3-6 Alice Yates (abt. 1860-aft. 1880) m. Manley Watts

3-7 John Morgan Yates (abt. 1863-aft. 1880) m. Annie
Huffman

3-8 William Leander Yates (abt. 1866-aft. 1880) m
Julia Cox Howard

3-9 Alpha Caroline Yates (abt. 1868-aft. 1880) m. Eli
McNeil

3-10 James Madison Yates (abt. 1869-1900) m. Pearl
Howard, Twin, to Thomas Jefferson Yates

3-11 Thomas Jefferson Yates (abt. 1870-1951) m.
Alpha Elizabeth Fletcher (abt. 1879-
aft 1930) d/o
William C Fletcher and Alpha J. Eller. He is a twin
to James Madison Yates.

3-12 Isaac Call Yates (abt. 1872-aft. 1880) m. Annie
Harmon

3-13 Presley C. Yates (abt. 1874-aft. 1900) m. Alice
Noland

2-7 Eli C. Yates (1820-bef 1887) m. 1) Nancy Spencer
(1830 d/o Solomon and Elenor Spencer 2) Rosemond
P. DeBord (1816-1890 d/o Reuben DeBord. Children of
Eli C. Yates and his 1st wife Nancy Spencer

3-1 Caroline Yates (1849, m. Charlie Phipps).

        4-1 Justin Phipps

        4-2 Rhoda Phipps

3-2 John Yates (abt 1851-bef 1870)

3-3 Elizabeth Yates (abt 1851-bef. 1870).

3-4 Lafayette Yates (abt. 1864)

3-5 Robert Yates (abt. 1869-1887).

Children of Eli C. Yates and his 2nd wife Rosemond

DeBord
    3-6 Birdie Nancy Yates (1871-1934 m. James Mitchell
        Neaves)
    3-7 Ludema Yates (abt, 1875 m. William Allen Neaves)
  2-8 Robert Yates (1822-1894) m. Jerusha Yates, his first
      cousin, d/o David Yates and Nancy Hayes. She was a
      sister of Sarahann and Adelaide Yates, the wives of the
      famous Siamese twins Chang and Eng
    3-1 Margaret Yates (abt. 1845-aft. 1850).
    3-2 Mary Yates (abt-1847-aft. 1850).
    3-3 Lafayette C. Yates (abt. 1849-aft. 1900)
    3-4 Josephine Yates (abt. 1859-aft.1900)
    3-5 Adelaide Yates (abt. 1862-aft. 1900)
    3-6 Decatur? Yates (abt. 1865-aft.1900)
    3-7 Belinda? Yates (abt. 1879-aft. 1900) (Is this a
        granddaughter?
        Children of John Yates, Jr. and his 2nd wife
        Fanny Lamira Laws
  2-9 Margaret Virginia Yates (1852-1864).
  2-10 Elizabeth Yates (1855-1948) m. Lowery Eller
      (1855-1812), Son of George Eller and Mary Minton
  2-11 Angeline Yates (1857-aft. 1880) m. Murchison
      Church (abt. 1858- aft 1880)
In 1880 Berryman Fletcher is living with Fanny's family. Beryman
Fletcher married her step-son's (Jesse's) daughter, Lulia A Yates in
1865 Lulia died before 1880.
  1-1 Robert Yates (1782- ?), Wilkes County, NC, m Mary
      Forester.
  1-2 Sarah Yates, (abt 1783 - ?) m. William Mitchell.
  1-3 Nancy Yates, (1785 - ?) m. George Wilcoxson
  1-4 Hugh Yates (Feb 05, 1786 at Lewis Fork, Wilkes,
      NC - July 13, 1871 at Ashe, NC) m. Sarah Vannoy
      (1785-aft. 1850), d/o Andrew Vannoy
    2-1 Jemima Yates (1809-1880) m. 1) William Phillips
        (1806-1857), (had18 children); 2) Isaac Brown
    2-2 John D. Yates (1811-1879) m. Alice Wilcox (Wilcoxson)

(abt. 1816-aft 1850)

3-1 James Yates 9abt 1842-aft 1850)

3-2 Robert Yates (abt. 1845-after. 1850).

3-3 Sarah Yates (abt. 1848-aft. 1850).

2-3 Couzanna Yates (1813-aft. 1860).

2-4 Frances Yates (1815-aft. 1850) m. John W. Whittington (abt. 892-aft.1850) (Found in the 1850 US Federal Census, Wilkes County, NC, is John Whittington, age 48 and his wife, Frances, age 36.)

Children in household:

3-1 Nelson Jones, age 16.

3-2 Martha Hynes (Hayes?) age 14.

3-4 Oregon D. Yates, age 3

2-5 Hugh Yates, Jr. (1818-aft. 1880) m. 1) Sarah Miller (?-bef. 1860) 2) Mrs. Emaline McGuire (abt. 1840-aft. 1880); 3) Lucinda Bradley (abt. 1827-abt. 1880).

(In the 1860 Federal Census Jobs Cabin, Wilkes Co., NC, Hugh Yates is living alone. Next door is Lucinda Bradley with children, Emeline, age 9; Martha, age 7, Esquire, age 5; and Claresey, age 1. They appear to be Bradley children, not Yates.)

(In the 1978-79 Federal Census Jobs Cabin, Wilkes Co., NC, Hugh Yates is living with Emeline, age 30— presumably this is Charity Emaline McGuire. Childen are Gordon Yates, age 13; Harvey Yates, age 10. Next door is Lucinda Bradley with children, Martha, age 16, Squire, age 13; and Carolina, age 10. (In the 1880 Federal Census Jobs Cabin, Wilkes Co., NC, Huge M. Yates, age 63, along with Charity E. Yates his wife, age 42. Children are James C. McGuire, age 22, identified as step-son; Harvie McGuire, 21, step-son; and Mary J. McGuire, age 18, step-daughter. Living next door is Lucinda Bradley, age 50. Children in her household are: Squire A. Yates, 21, son; and Martha M. A. Yates, 5, granddaughter.)

2-6 Sarah Isabelle Yates (1820) m. Thornton Kilby

2-7 Elizabeth Caroline Yates (1823) m. Hugh Hamby

2-8 Squire Allen Yates (1824-1895) m. Elizabeth Ann Miller
1-6 David Yates (abt. 1790, at Lewis Fork, Wilkes, NC-1851 at
    Wilkes, NC) m. 1) Nancy Hayes (abt. 1792-bef. 1850), d/o of
    Jesse Hayes and Nancy Ann Dickerson; 2) Millie Lunceford.
    2-1 Alston Yates (1816-1898) m. Elizabeth Holbrook (1838-
        1918), d/o Caleb Holbrook and Mary Winfrey
        3-1 Robert Pearce Yates (1860-1933) m. Martha Jane
            Phillips (1856-1945), d/o Elisha B Phillips and Mary
            Ferguson)
        3-2 Mary J. Yates m. John McGlamery
    2-2 Jesse Yates (1818-?)
    2-3 Letha Yates (1821-1910) m. Samuel J. Bauguess (aft
        1817-aft. 1850) (divorced in 1852)
        3-1 Robert
        3-2 Doctor
        3-3 Samuel
        3-4 James
    3-4 Sarahann Yates (Dec. 18, 1822-Apr 29, 1892) m. Eng
        Bunker, Siamese twin
        3-1 Katherine Marcellus Bunker, (Feb 10, 1844-
            August 15, 1871)
        3-2 Julia Ann Bunker, (March 31, 1845-February 27,
            1865)
        3-3 Stephen Decatur Bunker, (March 12, 1846-
            March 25, 1920)
        3-4 James Montgomery Bunker, (December, 16, 1848-
            April 24, 1921)
        3-5 Patrick Henry Bunker, (May 07, 1850-May 24, 1938,
            Medicine Lodge, KS)
        3-6 Roselyn Etta Bunker, (January 27, 1852 - February
            14, 1852)
        3-7 William Oliver Bunker, (January 31, 1855 – July
            15, 1932)
        3-8 Frederick Marshall Bunker, (February 01, 1857 –
            October 23, 1886)
        3-9 Rosella Virginia Bunker, (June 01, 1859 - October

09, 1941)

3-10 Georgianna Columbia Bunker (May 07, 1863 –
1865)

3-11 Robert Edmond Bunker, (April 17, 1865 – January
25, 1951)

2-5 Adelaide Yates (October 11, 1823-May 21, 1917) m.
Chang Bunker, Siamese twin

3-1 Josephine Virginia Bunker, (February 16, 1844 –
August 16, 1867)

3-2 Christopher Wren Bunker, (April 08, 1845 - April 02,
1932)

3-3 Nancy Adelaide Bunker, (June 05, 1847 - February
17, 1874)

3-4 Susan Mariana Bunker, (October 10, 1849 - March
02, 1922)

3-5 Victoria Bunker, (May 25, 1852 - November 15,
1896)

3-6 Louisa Emaline Bunker, (April 13, 1855 - March 30,
1934)

3-7 Albert Lemuel Bunker, (April 22, 1857 - October 8,
1944)

3-8 Jesse Lafayette Bunker, (April 07, 1861 - June 09,
1909)

3-9 Margaret Elizabeth Bunker, (October 06, 1863 –
November 03, 1950)

3-10 Hattie Irene Bunker, (September 12, 1868 –
November 16, 1945)

2-6 Jerusha Yates (1828-abt. 1900) m. Robert Yates,
her first cousin, s/o John Yates and Elizabeth Cleveland

1-7 Elizabeth Yates (1793 - 1794) Lewis Fork Wilkes Co., NC

1-8 Ann Yates (abt. 1792) m. William Turnbill

1-9 Louisa Yates, (1798 at Lewis Fork, Wilkes, NC) – m.
Abraham Johnson

1-10 Salvy Yates (1795 at Lewis Fork, Wilkes, NC, - 1869 at
Polk, TN), m Jacob Michael

1-11 Sarah Yates (1800) m, John Hamby

1-12 Tillman Yates (1802-1856 in NC) m. Mary Ann Bumgarner
 (abt. 1810- aft 1850)
　2-1 Elizabeth Yates m. Murphy Pilkenton
　2-2 George W. Yates (abt. 1834-aft. 1850).
　2-3 Louise Yates (abt. 1835-aft. 1850) m. Wesley Pilkenton
　2-4 Jemima Yates (abt. 1837-aft.1850).
　2-5 John David Yates (1840-1911) m. Clara Ann (Annie)
　　 Gamble, (moved to West Virginia)
　2-6 Jesse F. Yates (abt. 1841-aft. 1850).
　2-7 Permelia Yates (abt. 1843-aft. 1850).
　2-8 Leonard M. Yates (abt. 1847-aft. 1850).
　2-9 Tillman A. Yates (bef. 1856).

APPENDIX B

Who was Charles Harris?

Born 1801 - Died 1849...

Charles Harris was born in Dublin, Ireland, on January 6, 1801. He had become friends with James Hale while touring with the Bunker twins in England. Harris had come to America to "seek his fortune," and was living in a boardinghouse in Newburgh, New York. The friendship between Harris and Hale resumed. The two men corresponded fairly regular while Hale was touring with the twins. Apparently, at some point, Harris had shared with Hale that he was doing very poorly financially and was contemplating a return trip to England. Hale, being a very concerned friend, was very worried about Harris' shortage of finances, so Hale wrote Harris to offer him a loan of $100. Also, in this letter Hale expanded more on his future plans of leaving the management of Eng and Chang because he was not getting along well with Susan Coffin; he wanted to pursue another business venture, and also spend more time with his wife and children. Hale had already confided to Harris what these plans might be.

In the letter, Hale refreshed Harris on the current relationship between himself and his employer. Hale then told Harris that within seven months he was planning to purchase a tavern in Massachusetts, and work for himself. Hale also knew that Eng and Chang knew Harris, and they liked him. So when the time came for Hale to inform Susan Coffin of his plans to terminate his employment, he knew that a replacement would be needed immediately. Of course, Hale knew a very competent person that he could recommend, and also one who was available to take the job. Naturally, Hale recommended his friend, Charles Harris, to become the new manager of Eng and Chang.

Immediately, Harris came to meet and have his interview with Mrs. Coffin. The interview went well because immediately after the interview, a contract was signed between the two parties. There seemed to be a rather smooth transition in the management of Eng and Chang because they knew and liked Harris, and they cared about him.

Charles Harris was 30 years old when he began managing the Bunker twins. This was in October, 1831, and the twins would be turning 21 in 1832. Although he was a trained accountant, he listed himself as a doctor in a passport that had been obtained in 1835. As a result, the twins always addressed him as "Doctor."

Harris, being a prolific letter writer, literally bombarded the Coffins with correspondence, outlining every detail of the twins' travels, their business, their needs, and their activities. The twins were aware of the amount of money that was coming in, and also aware of how unfair Susan Coffin had been in paying them. So on their 21st birthday, realizing that in America they could declare their own independence, they did so. Eng and

Chang approached Susan Coffin, and broke all ties with her. They reminded her that they had fulfilled their initial contract of exhibiting under the supervision of the Coffins until their 21st birthday. They were now "Their Own Men."

The first act of business on their own was to retain the services of Charles Harris as their manager. They liked him, he knew his job, and they respected him. Harris was extremely fond of the twins, and he never had any reason to leave them. Now that the twins were in business for themselves and prepared to work even harder,
Harris found it necessary to keep two daily record books. One would consist of their earnings each month, and the other was a day-by-day listing of all money that was spent and how it was spent.

Over the next several years, the twins were very busy touring most of the United States and many foreign countries. When they were not on the road, they had become regulars at one of the four Peale's Museums located in the north. Once, when they were appearing at the museum in New York City, an event happened that would change their future forever. This was when they met Dr. James Calloway, a physician visiting New York from North Carolina. The doctor was very interested in the twins, and asked to meet them on a personal basis. Permission was granted.

In the course of their conversation, Dr. Calloway told the twins all about his hometown of Wilkesboro and the beauty that lay in the beautiful Blue Ridge Mountains, with great hunting and bountiful fishing in the streams. Then he invited the twins to come to his hometown for a visit, a vacation, a time to just relax. The twins, who had been on the road for about eight years, were ready for a long vacation. So after consulting with their manager, Charles Harris, it was agreed that they would accept the invitation and together the three would come to Wilkesboro for some free time.

The twins, along with Harris, rented rooms and extended their stay. The twins soon realized that they did not want to return to Siam. They did not want to go back to touring the United States. Wilkesboro was a different world to Eng and Chang. There was a feeling of peacefulness, a feeling of friendliness to the people. Local folks' handshakes felt firm and friendly, their smiles seemed sincere. When speaking, the people sounded honest and caring. This county had become the closest thing they had found to a haven, and they wanted to make it their home.

After making the decision to explore the possibility of remaining in the Wilkes County area, Harris, along with Eng and Chang, changed their temporary residence. They had located a home out in a remote area of Traphill that was owned by a merchant and farmer named Robert Bauguess. It just happened that Robert Bauguess had two rooms in his house that he was willing to rent. So Harris rented one, and Eng and Chang rented the other. As it turned out, this move altered the life of Charles Harris and Eng and Chang forever.

It just happened that Robert Bauguess had a daughter, Fannie Bauguess, whose charm immediately appealed to Harris and his heart instantly went out to her.

Most of the time, the twins had known Harris to be all business, but now, wanting to win the affection of Fannie Bauguess, he was quick with a joke and a laugh, and was always aware of how his humor affect the young daughter of his landlord. Harris was now 38, and he was beginning to speak of finding a wife and settling down. To no one's surprise, Fannie Bauguess was his choice. Within 10 months, a wedding was going to take place between Charles Harris and Fannie Bauguess.

With the word spreading over the community that a wedding would be taking place, it was a custom of the Wilkes County people that such events called for a celebration. There would not only be a ceremony, but also a grand wedding supper to follow.

The big day had finally arrived. The ceremony went very smoothly, as expected. Eng and Chang were a part of the ceremony, standing very close to the groom. Immediately following the ceremony, the wedding party and their guests were all seated to an elaborate meal that had been brought in from all parts of this county. The tables were "stacked" with platters of pork, venison, and pheasant with all of the trimmings. After the meal, there would be even more celebrating with everyone who brought their stringed instruments beginning to play music, and everyone dancing. It was apparent that the people of Wilkes County knew how to celebrate.

Apparently, romance was really in the air at this occasion. Very soon into the celebration, Eng and Chang caught sight of the two Yates sisters in a corner of the room. The sisters were Sarah, age 18, and Adelaide, age 17, both daughters of David Yates.

A courtship soon developed and all of this is discussed in Chapter 5.

St. Paul's Episcopal Church, Wilkesboro, NC

Charles Harris, meanwhile, recognizing a good thing when it presented itself, found a bride and settled down in the community. In June of 1839, he petitioned the Wilkes Superior court to become a naturalized citizen of the United States. Harris worked at store clerking, became a rural postmaster, and was said to have worked for St. Paul's Church. There is no record of him doing anything at the church. Harris is listed in the church register as a parishioner on January 2, 1848. According to the register, he died July 4, 1849, and was buried at the church a week before the new church was consecrated by Bishop Ives.

Where is his grave? No one has found it, but many have speculated. At least one member of this church guess was that Harris was buried under the church. I don't think so because the church was about finished when he died, and it would have been a whole lot easier just to place him in the ground outside. With no family to honor him, and no permanent marker to preserve his memory, Charles Harris's location in time was forgotten, not unlike others buried at St. Paul's with unmarked graves.

In summary, Charles Harris was no physician, but he was called "Doctor," or "Doc." He immigrated to America looking for a "better" life for himself. In New York, he attached himself to the touring showmen Siamese Twins and became their business manager. He was with them when a young medical student, James Calloway, attended one of their performances in New York, and fascinated by the unique fusion of the twins, he visited them backstage. Chang and Eng told him they cherished a pastoral life with opportunities for hunting and fishing, and Calloway told them about his home town and the surrounding unspoiled foothills. The twins resolved to come and see for themselves. They arranged a performance at Wilkesboro School on June 7, 1837, and liked the community and the charms of the Wilkes country side. This was where the Siamese Twins decided to retire from show business, and they moved here and bought a farm near Traphill, married two local sisters, and raised large family.

Charles Harris Family

Charles Harris was married Frances (called Fanny Bauguess), on November 3, 1839. She was the daughter of Robert Bauguess. They were married by George W. Smoat, Esq. Fannie was born on March 17, 1818 and died November 19, 1891, at 5 o'clock A.M. She had a chew of tobacco in her mouth when she died and no one knows where she got it. (This was copied from the family bible.)

Charles and Fanny lived in Wilkesboro for a while, and then moved to Traphill, where they bought 150 acres of land from Robert Bauguess (Fanny's father). The Siamese twins bought the first tract of land, and Charles bought the second tract.

Charles Harris only lived 10 years after he married. He contacted tuberculosis, and within two months he died on July 05, 1849. He is reportedly buried under the doorstep of the St. Paul's Episcopal Church in Wilkesboro, North Carolina.

Six Children:
1. A still born female, March 24, 1841
2. Joseph T Harris, born June 17, 1842, and died September 24, 1903, in Gridley, California. Married Martha Corrender, November 12 1865, in Wilkes County, NC
3. John R. Harris born December 1, 1845 and died December 3, 1845
4. Maryann Almeda Harris was born March 12, 1846. She died July 24, 1908. Married D. Layayette, (Fayet) McBride March 8, 1866. Fayet was a Confederate soldier, 54th Regiment, enlisted September 10, 1862. He was born 1845.
5. Sarah Jane Harris born October 19, 1848. Died November 30, 1939, Wilkes County, NC. Married Martin Green McBride, February 15, 1866. He was the son of John J. McBride and Rachel Curry Gray. He was born November 06, 1844, and died September 27, 1924 in Wilkes County, NC
6. Columbus Lafayette Last Name Unknown, born February 10, 1856, died September 22, 1862 in Traphill Township, Wilkes County, North Carolina.

Children of Sarah Jane Harris and Martin Green McBride
1. Frances Victoria McBride married John Quincy Adams Brown
2. Joseph Tyre McBride married Margaret Yale

3. Maryann Almeda McBride born May 18, 1873, died November 15, 1953,   married John T. Miles
4. John Robins McBride married Ida Spicer
5. Robert William McBride married Mary Lunina Edwards
6. James Walter McBride married Myrtle Bryann
7. Martin Edgar married Maude Laray Spicer
8. Charles Quincy married (1) Kizzie F.; (2) Pearl Brown

Maryann Almeda McBride and John T. Miles are the grandparents of this writer, Melvin M. Miles. This makes Charles Harris my great great grandfather.

Old Episcopal Church in Wilkesboro, North Carolina. Charles Harris helped to build this church in the 1840's. He died shortly before the construction was completed. He is believed to be buried somewhere on the church property without a marker. It was a personal request from Mr. Harris to not have a marker at his grave.

APPENDIX C

Siamese Twins were Good Farmers

World Famous pair became North Carolina planters one hundred years ago.

- **Almost everybody the whole world around has heard of the "Siamese Twins," Eng and Chang Bunker. But how many know that 100 years ago this year this world famous pair became progressive Southern farmers and slaveholders and remained so till 1865—two of the most famous planters who ever lived in Dixie?**

WHO were the most famous men who have ever farmed in North Carolina in its 300 years of history?

Ask any Southern farmer outside of North Carolina and he will not know. Ask 99 out of 100 North Carolina farmers and they will not know.

Go almost anywhere on earth and ask, "Have you heard of the Siamese twins?" And the answer will be, "Yes." But go even within 100 miles of where they long lived as Southern slaveholder planters, and this fact about their careers has been strangely forgotten.

Eng and Chang, or "the Siamese Twins" as they have become known to the four corners of the earth, were born at Bauguess, Siam, May 11, 1811. Their bodies strangely united by a cartilaginous band that surgeons dared not cut apart, the twins were exhibited all over the world from the ages of about 20 to 30.

To "Get Away from it All"

But 100 years ago this year, weary of travel and the start of the curious and having amassed a fortune, the Twins sought quiet and recreation in the lordly Blue Ridge Mountains of North Carolina. It was in 1839. They hunted and fished, then repeatedly extended their season of hunting and fishing; they stayed on and on in the majestic hills of the Southern highlands, where t hey were completely apart from the seething crowds pertinent to their life as "The Colossal and Astounding Vagary of Nature's Handiwork," as they were termed by their exhibitors in the show business. Soon they were the proprietors of a large general store away back in the seclusion of Wilkes County and of broad acres of land. They went in for farming in a big way.

Eng and Chang also put thousands of dollars into slaves and became the first citizens of the county. Hitherto they had had no names other than Eng and Chang. The state Legislature, however remedied things by authorizing the Twins to adopt the surname of Bunker.

House Still Stands

Today, not far from the route of the Scenic Parkway stands an old weather beaten house, a forlorn monument to the day romance led the world-weary Siamese Twins—young and handsome, and, for their day, fabulously wealthy, to wedlock with the charming Yates sisters, daughters of a wealthy planter and slaveholder. Eng married Sara Yates, Chang married Adelaide.

Eng and Chang Bunker, as they were now called, sold their general store and removed to White Plains, Surry County. There they owned everything in common for several years and were very happy. But domestic troubles soon came about and eventually, after the births of several children, the wives clamored for separate homes. How the Twins, inseparably bound by nature, could live in two homes was a problem. They finally decided to establish two domiciles, however, spending half of the week in each one.

The Siamese Twins advocated and put into effect on their large plantation much that the farmer of today calls scientific farming. They read farm literature and used improved methods. Cleaning their broad acres of stones, brush, etc., they fertilized it and built it up by ditching, deep plowing, and turning under clover and peas. They studied the new farm implements and introduced several into Surry County, enticing the landowners from along the Yadkin to make a visit of inspection. They bought improved cattle and sheep, and were careful f their comfort and saw to their good treatment. Among the first men in the state to produce bright tobacco, they had a tobacco press where the slaves manufactured chewing tobacco.

But just as the plantation as becoming famous, yielding a bounty in varied crops, along came the Emancipation Proclamation, leaving them disheartened and broken. Their 75 slaves emancipated, and their fortunes depleted, the Twins found it necessary to go on a world tour and make personal exhibitions, distasteful though it was to them.

In 1869, after a world tour with Barnum's Circus, Chang suffered a paralytic stroke while en route home from Liverpool, England. January 17, 1874, while the Twins lay sleeping Chang died from his second paralytic stroke. Eng lived only a few hours. Today in the village cemetery of White Plains, N.C., almost under the rim of the great Blue Ridge Mountains near to their final resting place.

Copied from the Progressive Farmer (Magazine), November 1939, by HARRY A. TUCKER

REFERENCE

Works Essential to my Research

PUBLICATIONS

Life Magazine, National Geographic Magazine, June, 2006; Mount Airy News, Mount Airy Times, Our State Magazine, Progressive Farmer, November, 1939; Tampa Bay Times, Dec.26, 2012; Southern, St. John Episcopal Church of Wilkesboro, NC; White Plains Baptist Church Brochure.

PERSONAL INTERVIEWS

Betty Bunker Blackmon, Jessie Bunker Bryant, Dean and Dee Hodges, (Current Owners of the Original Home of Eng and Chang in Traphill, NC), Tanya Blackmon Jones, Vena Miles Newsome, Donna G. Smith, Bonnie Robertson Pino, Deidre Blackmon Rodgers, Various members of Yates Family, and members of Surry County Genealogical Society.

PHOTOGRAPHS

Betty Bunker Blackmon, Dean Hodges and Dee Hodges, Personal Collection of author Melvin M. Miles, Sarah Beamer Nixon from Album of her Great Grandmother, Kitty Beamer, Surry Arts Council, Siamese Photo Exhibit

BOOKS

Bryant, Jessie Bunker - The Connected Bunkers.
Winston Salem, Jostens, 2001.
Collins, David - Eng & Chang The Original Siamese Twins.
New York, Dillon Press, 1994.
Hunter, Kay - Duet for a Lifetime. New York, Coward McCann, 1984.
Slouka Mark - God's Fool. New York, Random House, Inc., 2002.
Strauss, Darin- Chang and Eng. New York, Penguin Putman Inc., 2000.
Wallace, Irving and Amy Wallace -The Two.
New York, Simon and Schuster, 1978

LIBRARIES AND ORGANIZATIONS

Mount Airy Public Library, Surry Community College Library, Genealogy Room, Wilkes County Public Library, Surry Arts Council, Mount Airy, NC; Surry County Genealogy Society, University Of North Carolina, Wilson Library.

Dean and DeAnn Hodges

      Dean and DeAnn Hodges moved to North Carolina from Michigan and are the proud new owners of the original house built by Eng and Chang Bunker on Longbottom Road in Traphill, North Carolina. This house was built in the 1830's. The new owners are happy to extend an invitation to any of the Bunker descendants and their families to come by for a visit. Please contact them at the address below to arrange a visit:

14016 Longbottom Road
Traphill, NC 28685

      Both Dean and DeAnn are interested in meeting the descendants and learning all the history they possibly can about these very famous brothers, their wives and their families.

A note upon finishing my first book...

Now that you have traveled with me, the writer, on the journey of Eng and Chang from their birth on a bamboo mat in Bangkok, Siam, to their final resting place in Surry County, North Carolina, it is my desire that you, the reader, have found the journey to be not only educational but also fascinating... with the birth, the childhood, the traveling, the marriage, the 21 children, and the grand exit from life. Even after their death the twins did not truly rest until being placed in their 4th and final burial.

The spirit of the original "World Famous Siamese Twins" continues to live throughout the world and it is the hope of this writer that reading "From Siam to Surry" will only broaden this base.

Special Thanks to:

Abreena W. Tompkins, EdD - Editor
Donna G. Smith - Cover Design & Formatting

About the Author

Melvin Miles is a retired high school teacher who enjoys talking with fans of The Andy Griffith Show as well as those interested in Mount Airy's Siamese Twins. He has volunteered every weekend for the past two years in the Siamese Twins Exhibit on the lower level of the Andy Griffith Playhouse. Melvin is a squad car tour driver and local history advocate during the weekdays. He has spoken at the annual Bunker Reunion for the past three years and is a regular attendee. He speaks to genealogy, civic, and school groups on the Siamese Twins and other topics of local interest. We are grateful for his interest and his many volunteer hours at the Surry Arts Council.

Tanya Jones
Executive Director, Surry Arts Council
Great-Great-Granddaughter of Eng Bunker

Notes of Interest

Vice Admiral Terry M. Cross

*Terry Michael Cross assumed the duties as Vice Commandant of the United States Coast Guard from July 2004 until June 2006.1 He served as the Coast Guard's second in command and was the Agency Acquisition Executive.

Cross graduated from the Coast Guard Academy in 1970 with a BS degree in Engineering. He also earned a master's degree in Industrial Administration from Purdue University's Krannert School of Management and is a graduate of the National War College.

Vice Admiral Cross retired on 1 August 2006. He was a great-great-grandson to Eng Bunker and a great-grandson to Robert Edward Bunker, grandson of Lucian Edgar Cross and Katherine "Kate" Marcellus Bunker Cross, and son of Lucian Edgar Cross, Jr. and Martha Jo DeCamp.

*As of 2003 Nancy Louise Bunker Ward is the only living grandchild of the Eng-Chang families. She is a granddaughter of Chang Bunker. Nancy was born February 16, 1925 in Surry County, NC to Albert Lemuel an Nina Angel Bunker. Presently she lives at Plymouth, NC.

*George Franklin Ashby (1885-1950), was the son of George Whitfield and Rosella Virginia Bunker Ashby. He was the President of Union Pacific Railroad in 1946. Also he was the grandson of Eng Bunker.

*As of this writing, 2013, the surname "Bunker" is completely exhausted in Chang Bunkers lineage.

Author Melvin M. Miles presents
H. E. Dr. Chaiyong Satjipanon,
The Royal Thai Ambassador,
with a copy of his debut book
"From Siam To Surry"
July 27, 2013

Notes

Notes

<u>Notes</u>